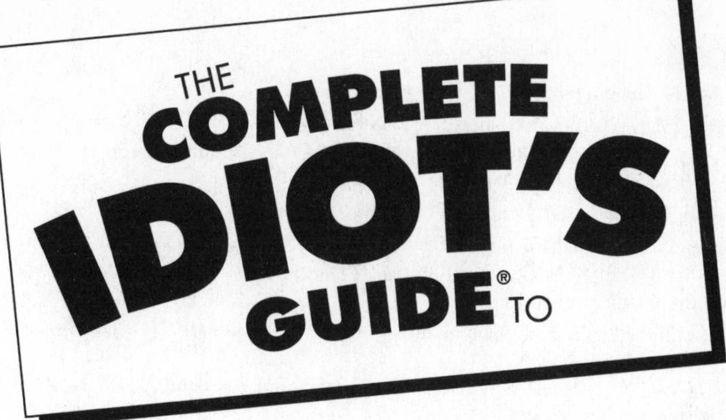

Sushi and Sashimi

by James O. Fraioli with Chef Kaz Sato

A member of Penguin Group (USA) Inc.

ALPHA BOOKS

Published by the Penguin Group

Penguin Group (USA) Inc., 375 Hudson Street, New York, New York 10014, USA

Penguin Group (Canada), 90 Eglinton Avenue East, Suite 700, Toronto, Ontario M4P 2Y3, Canada (a division of Pearson Penguin Canada Inc.)

Penguin Books Ltd, 80 Strand, London WC2R 0RL, England

Penguin Ireland, 25 St. Stephen's Green, Dublin 2, Ireland (a division of Penguin Books Ltd.)

Penguin Group (Australia), 250 Camberwell Road, Camberwell, Victoria 3124, Australia (a division of Pearson Australia Group Pty. Ltd.)

Penguin Books India Pvt. Ltd., 11 Community Centre, Panchsheel Park, New Delhi—110 017, India

Penguin Group (NZ), 67 Apollo Drive, Rosedale, North Shore, Auckland 1311, New Zealand (a division of Pearson New Zealand Ltd.)

Penguin Books (South Africa) (Pty.) Ltd, 24 Sturdee Avenue, Rosebank, Johannesburg 2196, South Africa

Penguin Books Ltd., Registered Offices: 80 Strand, London WC2R 0RL, England

International Standard Book Number: 978-1-59257-782-8
Library of Congress Catalog Card Number: 2008920830

10 09 08 8 7 6 5 4 3 2 1

Interpretation of the printing code: The rightmost number of the first series of numbers is the year of the book's printing; the rightmost number of the second series of numbers is the number of the book's printing. For example, a printing code of 08-1 shows that the first printing occurred in 2008.

Printed in the United States of America

Publisher: *Marie Butler-Knight*
Editorial Director: *Mike Sanders*
Senior Managing Editor: *Billy Fields*
Acquisitions Editor: *Michele Wells*
Development Editor: *Julie Bess*
Production Editor: *Megan Douglass*
Copy Editor: *Nancy Wagner*
Cartoonist: *Shannon Wheeler*
Cover Designer: *Bill Thomas*
Book Designer: *Trina Wurst*
Indexer: *Johnna Vanhoose Dinse*
Layout: *Ayanna Lacey*
Proofreader: *Mary Hunt*

Contents at a Glance

Contents

Introduction

Today, sushi and sashimi are enjoyed around the globe, and in the United States the delectable cuisine continues to grow in popularity. What exactly are sushi and sashimi? This short description and history should get you up to speed.

Sushi is defined as a combination of raw fish and vinegared rice, whose origin dates back to China and Southeast Asia where fish and rice fermentation dishes still exist today. In Japan, the oldest form of sushi is known as *Narezushi*, in which the fish was preserved for months before being eaten while the rice was thrown out. During the Muromachi period (1336–1573) of Japan, vinegar was added to the rice for better taste and both fish and rice began to be consumed together. By the mid-eighteenth century, sushi was being crafted in bamboo molds and sold as shapely bite-size edibles in Tokyo. But the real contemporary version, internationally known as "sushi," was actually invented by Hanaya Yohei (1799–1858) at the end of the Edo period. The sushi Hanaya invented was an early form of fast food that was not fermented—therefore prepared quickly—and could be eaten with the hands, eliminating utensils all together. Originally, this sushi was known as *Edomae zushi* because it used freshly-caught fish in Tokyo Bay. Though the fish used in modern sushi no longer comes from Tokyo Bay, it is still formally known as *Edomae nigirizushi.*

Sashimi, on the other hand, is simply defined as slices of raw fish. Sashimi is served without the rice and has probably been around since the dawn of man.

We will explore both sushi and sashimi throughout the pages of this culinary book, along with 70 mouth-watering recipes for you to try at home. To assist you, we've included advice from a professional sushi chef who will be by your side every step of the way.

How This Book Is Organized

This book is divided into two parts:

In **Part 1: "The Basics,"** Chef Kaz Sato of Kai Suchi in Santa Barbara, California, will teach you everything you need to know to start making delicious sushi and sashimi at home. We begin with an introduction to a bevy of seafood items available in today's marketplace. We offer tips and suggestions on purchasing this seafood and how to properly store your fresh fish at home. In Chapter 2, Chef Sato offers advice and suggestions when shopping for fresh fruits and vegetables, along with the necessary bottled and dry goods. After we've presented needed ingredients, we then run through the basics of setting up your own sushi kitchen. These include the essential equipment you'll need to make great-tasting sushi and sashimi, as well as simple kitchen gadgets that can make your life a lot easier. Finally, before the actual sushi and sashimi making begins, we give you a crash course on making the all-important ingredient in Japanese cuisine—sushi rice—and explain in detail how to slice and dice your ingredients. We wrap up this section with an introductory course on how to cut a whole fish down to more manageable pieces.

After you feel comfortable and confident with the basics, we give you more than 70 delicious sushi and sashimi recipes to try at home in **Part 2: "The Recipes."** From Sashimi à la Carte, such as sliced halibut, tuna, and yellowtail, to salmon, octopus, and surf clam sushi, the recipes are extremely quick and easy to follow. As your culinary skills increase, you can move on to making the various sushi rolls, from the classic California roll to the colorful and creative Caterpillar and Rainbow Rolls. You'll find a good selection of cooked and tempura rolls, followed by exclusive recipes for the vegetarian and a collection of appetizers and salads to use when you host your own sushi dinner party.

Throughout the pages, you will discover plenty of interesting facts and Did-you-Know? sidebars. These will help educate you on the wonderful world of sushi while enjoying the delicious bounty of the sea. So what are you waiting for? Turn the pages and begin your gastronomic adventure.

Fish Facts

Not everyone is an expert when it comes to identifying the creatures that dwell beneath the sea. The Fish Facts box provides educational tid-bits to better acquaint you with popular seafoods used in sushi and sashimi.

Food Corner

Learn more about various ingredients by reading notes from the Food Corner. Interesting facts are interspersed throughout the book to arm you with a greater culinary knowledge.

From the Kitchen

Need helpful pointers and insider tips from a professional sushi chef along the way? This box is your solution to making sushi and sashimi even more fun and simple.

Acknowledgments

James O. Fraioli and Chef Kaz Sato would like to thank literary agent Andrea Hurst, attorney James Ballantine, and the many patrons who continue to support Kai Sushi. Chef Sato would like to personally thank his son Kai for giving him the inspiration, love, and patience to take his career to another level and make him the person he is today.

Trademarks

Part 1

The Basics

In this part, you'll learn everything you need to know to produce delicious sushi and sashimi, from choosing the right seafood to finding other ingredients. You'll also receive a crash-course in preparing sushi rice.

Chapter 1

The Key Ingredients

In This Chapter

- Twenty-five popular seafoods for sushi and sashimi
- Did you Know? fish facts
- Selecting and caring for your catch

Navigating the Waters

You don't know tako from tuna or what tako even is (no, not the favorable Mexican dish misspelled)! When learning about sushi and sashimi, you may be bombarded with unfamiliar terms, such as this. But don't worry. There's no need to panic or consult a marine biologist to help you understand every critter dwelling beneath the sea.

You'll be pleased to know that a relatively short inventory of fish and shellfish appear in sushi cuisine because the seafood used is unlike what you find displayed on ice at your local supermarket. For sushi and sashimi, only sushi-grade is used. Sushi–grade is an industry term for high-quality seafood suitable for eating raw. High-quality is defined as freshly caught seafood that is properly handled and processed for sushi consumption.

To be well informed when ordering or preparing sushi or sashimi, you need to familiarize yourself with the popular players, so we've showcased the top twenty-five for you. And to make it even easier, we've included both the American and Japanese name, along with a brief description to eliminate any guesswork of what's about to slide down your gullet.

Fin Fish

Fin fish means exactly that: fish with fins. The following are the common fin fish served as sushi and sashimi. When transforming into a Japanese chef, the most important rule to remember is to buy fresh. If your favorite fish did not arrive from sea to store in several days, choose another species that did.

Albacore *(Shiro maguro)*

Albacore is a medium-size tuna inhabiting the world's temperate, subtropical, and tropical waters. Distinguished by its long, graceful pectoral fins, the albacore is the only "white meat" tuna. Its flesh ranges from rose to pale peach in color, and its flavor is rich but not overbearing. Because albacore meat is soft, difficult to handle, and quickly changes color, some sushi chefs choose not to serve this species.

Fish Facts

Albacore can accumulate more mercury than other kinds of tuna. Traditionally, long-line albacore are older fish which have high levels of mercury. To avoid such metals, request the younger albacore which are often troll-caught.

Freshwater Eel *(Unagi)*

The freshwater eel or Japanese eel is actually a fish that dwells in shallow waters and spends its time hiding in caverns. The eel's elongated body is a sushi bar favorite because it is all meat with little waste. Often prepared and broiled, eel meat is high in protein, vitamin A, calcium, cholesterol, and saturated fat.

Flying Fish Roe *(Tobiko)*

This highly prized roe comes from the flying fish, a marine species with unusually large fins which enable it to escape predators by taking short gliding flights through the air. The fish's orange or red colored eggs are small, crunchy, and often used to enhance the flavor, texture, and presentation of many sushi dishes. It is typically found on the inside, outside, or as a topping of sushi rolls.

Halibut *(Hirame)*

Halibut is the largest of all flatfish. They live in both the North Pacific and the North Atlantic oceans and spend their time camouflaged on the ocean bottom waiting for prey. A highly regarded food fish, smaller-size halibut are preferred for sushi due to their moist white meat and mild flavor.

Fish Facts

Halibut weighing more than 100 pounds are often called Whales or Barn Doors while halibut less than 20 pounds are called Chickens—the ideal size for sushi.

Mackerel *(Saba)*

The mackerel is a slim, cylindrical shape fish found in all tropical and temperate seas. They are often harvested for their meat, which is typically very oily. In Japan, mackerel are farm-raised and specifically prepared for sushi and sashimi. Because the meat can spoil quickly, mackerel is the only common salt-cured sushi.

Sea Bream, a.k.a. Red Snapper *(Tai)*

Bream is a general term for a number of species of freshwater and marine fish that tend to be narrow with deep bodies. Also called red snapper in sushi kitchens, bream is some of the best-tasting and most nutritious of all white-meat fish. Because of its popularity, bream is now cultivated in man-made ponds and waterbeds; however, bream caught in the ocean tends to have better taste.

Salmon *(Sake)*

Salmon are robust, deep-bodied silvery fish, which are anadromous: they live in the sea and enter freshwater to spawn. Since salmon are part freshwater fish, they can be susceptible to parasites and should be cured by salting prior to consumption. Larger salmon are generally used for sushi and sashimi due to their higher fat/oil content.

Fish Facts

The U. S. market is flooded with inexpensive farmed salmon. Whenever possible, buy wild-caught salmon, particularly from Alaska. Alaskan salmon have healthy and abundant populations, and are by far the better alternative.

Salmon Roe *(Ikura)*

The large and bright orange salmon eggs are often harvested from wild salmon from Alaskan and Canadian waters. After harvest, the roe is processed and cured, allowing its briny flavor to shine through. Salmon roe is a popular topping, filling, and garnishment for sushi.

Smelt Roe *(Masago)*

Masago is the roe from the smelt fish, a small anadromous species like the salmon that runs in large schools along the coastline during its spawning migration. The smelt family consists of some sixteen species whose eggs are highly prized. Smelt roe is often found in sushi and sashimi where the bright color and mild flavor of the tiny eggs enhance the dish.

Tuna *(Maguro)*

This tuna, the yellowfin tuna, is an open-water fish found in warm oceans except the Mediterranean. Its sashimi-grade meat is deep red and often sold as succulent loins, cut from the tail end of the loin first, with no bones. In Hawaii, the tuna's red meat is called ahi. In Japan, it is maguro. Fattier yellowfin tuna is often preferred delicious by itself as sashimi or prepared in sushi rolls.

Tuna Belly, Fatty *(Toro)*

In Japan, tuna is graded and priced according to fat content, and the fattiest part of the fish is the most prized. Often the most expensive item on a sushi menu, toro is the section you want. Toro is cut from the tuna's belly and may be pink and somewhat opaque. Many sushi chefs identify toro as either chutoro, which is moderately fat, or otoro, which indicates the highest fat content.

Yellowtail *(Hamachi)*

Yellowtail is the common name for a number of species of amberjack—sleek migratory fish similar to the tunas. But do not confuse yellowtail with yellowfin tuna, two completely different species. Much consumed yellowtail is wild-caught, but amberjack is now being farm-raised for sushi and sashimi.

Shellfish

Shellfish is a generic term used to describe various nonfin fish, so we've decided to group the shrimp, prawn, and the most popular crab species in this category. Unlike most fin-fish, shellfish, particularly crab, are often delivered to the market live or cooked.

Shrimp & Prawns *(Ebi)*

Shrimp and prawns (very large shrimp) are long-bodied crustaceans that thrive on ocean floors around the world. Judging from the enormous amount consumed each year, shrimp and prawns remain America's most popular shellfish. Their meaty texture, lack of bones, and ready-to-eat convenience contribute to their popularity. Shrimp and prawns prepared for sushi are always a customer favorite and are found in many sushi rolls.

Snow Crab *(Kani)*

Snow Crab, also called opilio or tanner crab, is a large spider-like crab commonly taken from the icy waters of Alaska's Bering Sea. Noted for its sweet, delicate flavor, snow-white meat, and tender texture, snow crab is ideal for sushi rolls.

Soft Shell Crab *(Kani)*

Soft shell crabs are actually blue crabs and sometimes Mangrove crabs in parts of Asia. These crabs are harvested during their molting stage when they shed their hard exterior shell. This allows for the entire crab to be consumed. Fried quickly until crisp, soft shell crabs are popular by themselves or prepared in sushi rolls.

King Crab *(Kani)*

King Crabs are characterized by their massive size, long spidery legs, spiny exteriors, and reoccurring appearance on Discovery Channel's *The Deadliest Catch.* Often harvested from Alaskan waters, king crabs are prized for their immense sweet meat, which is cleaned and cooked before reaching the market.

Fish Facts

Due to reduced Alaskan seasons, much of the king crab catch is made in Russian and international waters by large crab processors.

Mollusks & Others

Mollusks are often grouped under the shellfish category, but we've given these marine edibles their own section. A mollusk, for those who are unfamiliar, is a term used for various clams, mussels, squid, and octopus. Although some are freshwater species, the majority of mollusks consumed are of the saltwater variety.

Abalone *(Awabi)*

Abalone is a large marine snail with a beautiful mother-of-pearl shell and a large muscular foot for attaching itself to rocky surfaces. The foot is one of the best tasting seafoods. The rich opaque meat is removed from the shell, cleaned and rinsed, and sliced into portions. Because of the depletion of wild populations, farm-raised abalone is now the choice for this luxury seafood.

Cockle *(Torigai)*

The cockle is the common name for bivalve (two-shell) mollusks with distinct rounded shells that are heart-shaped and feature strongly pronounced ribs. The purple-gray color of the cockle's edible part—a characteristic feature as well as its taste and unique texture—makes cockles a popular delicacy in sushi bars and restaurants.

Oyster *(Kaki)*

Oysters are large mollusks with rough, fluted shells and a creamy-white flesh that has a unique dusky flavor. Oysters grow wild wherever they can find firm footing to support their weight. Aquaculturists also grow them on strings or nets to relieve the pressure on wild populations. Oysters often get their specific tastes from the areas in which they grow and are commonly sold under these place names.

Jellyfish *(Kurage)*

The blue jellyfish and the cannonball jellyfish—both possessing large bells and stinging tentacles—are two species of edible jellyfish which drift in massive numbers during summer months. Following harvest, jellyfish are immediately cleaned, salted, and dried in multiple stages to remove moisture. Jellyfish is a highly regarded delicacy in Japan where over 40 percent of jellyfish production is consumed.

Octopus *(Tako)*

An octopus is a highly mobile predator, which uses its eight suction-cup arms and a jet propulsion to dart across the bottom of the sea and capture prey, typically at night. Small octopus are cooked and blanched to ensure a white firm meat with sweet, mild flavor. Sliced tentacles are perfect for sashimi while the tentacle end pieces work well in sushi rolls.

Fish Facts

Since octopus mature within one year and have relatively short life spans—about 18 months—they are a very short-lived seafood item.

Scallop *(Hotategai)*

Scallops have two round shells held together by a small hinge and a large adductor muscle, which is the edible part of the scallop. Scallop meat should always be ivory or cream-colored and a bit sticky to the touch. The large sea scallop, known as the giant scallop or King of Scallops, is the preferred species for sushi.

Sea Urchin *(Uni)*

A relative of the starfish, sea urchins are spiny, hard-shelled animals that live on rocky seafloors where they use their long spines for moving and protection. Urchins are harvested for their roe, or uni, which appear as five yellow-orange strips arranged in a star-shaped pattern. Known for its sweet flavor and delicate texture, uni is sold according to freshness, color, shape, firmness, and taste and can command quite a price.

Squid *(Ika)*

Squid are voracious-eating cephalopods with a cigar-shaped body, two triangular fins, eight arms, and two feeding tentacles. After harvest, squid are brought on shore, pumped into totes, and a portion of their prized white meat is processed for sushi or sashimi. Squid meat is noted for its tender texture and sweet, mild flavor.

Surf Clam *(Hokkigai)*

Surf clams are large triangular-shape clams. They can grow up to six inches long and live in the surf zone, where the waves break. The adductor muscle of this clam is a delicious treat when formed into sushi and wrapped with a thin piece of roasted seaweed (nori). Surf clam is also a popular sashimi seafood.

Seafood Buying Tips

Shopping for seafood can be like browsing for a new car; you peruse the lot until you spot something that catches your eye. You approach the vehicle and examine its exterior, noting any visible flaws. Then you peek inside, giving the interior a good smell. Before you speak with a salesman, you compare the price of your selection with other similar models.

At the supermarket or fish stand, you often encounter a bevy of seafood displayed over ice. The fish may be whole or in trimmed and filleted sections, from wild-caught varieties to those strictly farm-raised, and cards may indicate which fish are from the United States and which are imported from other countries.

First, before you chose your fish, ask questions. Find out which seafood you should purchase as a wild-caught variety, and which should be farm-raised. For the more ethically minded, learn the difference between seafood harvested in U.S. waters and those brought in from overseas. All these elements play a vital role in purchasing the best and freshest seafood available.

To educate yourself about the fascinating world of seafood, visit the Monterey Bay Aquarium's Seafood Watch Program—a leader in informing the public about the ever-changing seafood industry at: www.montereybayaquarium.com/cr/seafoodwatch.asp.

After receiving a little education and finding that delicious fish you are eager to prepare for your family and friends, follow these helpful seafood-buying tips before you make your purchase:

- Seafood should never smell fishy. In fact, fresh fish should never have any unusual or offensive odor whatsoever. Always ask to smell the fish before you buy it. Don't wait until you're home to discover the seafood you bought is spoiled. This tip refers not only to buying fresh fish but also all seafood, including shrimp, prawns, scallops, and squid.

- If the fish you like still has the head intact, take a moment and inspect the eye, which should always be clear. A cloudy eye is a sign the fish is not fresh or has been previously frozen. The same holds true with the gills. They should be bright red. Pink or brown gills indicate a mishandled fish or one that has already spoiled.
- Inspect the flesh or meat. Fresh seafood should be firm and spring back when touched. If your finger leaves an impression, the meat is soft and has probably spoiled.
- Examine the skin of the fish. The exterior should be clean, and if any fins are intact, they should look crisp and moist, not discolored or dry, particularly around the edges.
- For clams, crabs, mussels, oysters, and the like, buy live whenever possible, rather than prepackaged products. This ensures the freshest quality.
- When buying live clams, mussels, and oysters, the shells should be tightly closed. If they are open, they should close when you touch them. They should also be housed in circulating seawater. If they are displayed on ice, make sure they are very cold—and alive.
- Live crabs and lobsters should also be stored in a circulating marine tank. These critters should be lively, especially when removed from the water. Do not purchase those that are limp and lifeless. If buying cooked crab or lobster, examine the shell. The exterior should be free of cracks and smell clean and fresh.

Food Corner

According to the National Fisheries Institute, the average American eats more than 15 pounds of seafood every year. Eating seafood rich in Omega-3 fatty acids at least twice a week benefits the hearts of healthy people, as well as those at high risk of cardiovascular disease.

Seafood Care

Seafood is different from other types of food because freshness is the key for safety and flavor. To ensure that you and your family and friends will enjoy the best sushi and sashimi possible, always remember these helpful pointers:

- If you purchase frozen seafood, keep it frozen until you are ready to eat it. To properly thaw, defrost fish in the refrigerator and never at room temperature. Also, plan ahead, as you may need to defrost a day before your dinner party.
- After purchasing fresh seafood, remove the wrapping from the market and transfer the fish to an airtight container or onto a plate covered with plastic wrap. If you are refrigerating more than one kind of seafood, do not store them together in one container or plate, and don't let the juices from one seafood come in contact with another.
- Live seafood, like clams, mussels, and oysters, cannot be frozen, but they should last for a couple days if you keep them on ice in a cool dark place. Note: do not cover the live seafood with ice as marine seafoods will quickly die in freshwater. Also remember that live seafood needs air to breathe, so remove them from the bag or container they were sold in. Cook live crab and lobster the same day you purchase them.
- If traveling a good distance, have the supermarket or fishmonger add a bag of ice with your seafood purchase. Your fresh fish must stay cold if you want it to remain fresh.
- If you are going to remember one rule when it comes to caring for your seafood, remember this one: consume fresh seafood the day you purchase it. The longer it sits, the quicker it spoils, as most fresh seafood has already been in transit four to six days before it reaches the market.

Although we introduced you to 25 of the most popular fish for sushi and sashimi, along with how to select and care for your purchase, dozens more seafood delights are available for you to try. Feel free to experiment, try other fish, and see what you like best. But regardless of what you choose, always buy from a reliable source, and always buy fresh whenever possible.

The Least You Need to Know

- Always purchase fresh seafood for sushi and sashimi, never frozen (flash-frozen is okay).
- Enjoy the seafood the day you purchase it; the longer it sits, the quicker it spoils.
- Never freeze live seafood; rather store on ice in a cool, dark place.

Chapter 2

Additional Ingredients

In This Chapter

- Popular fruits and vegetables
- Japanese specialty items
- The bottled and dry goods

Aside from the various seafood needed for sushi and sashimi, you will want to stock up on a number of other items which will accompany your delicious dishes. Most, if not all, of these items are available at your local grocer, but for those items that are not, take a quick search on the Internet and have these products delivered right to your doorstep.

A point worth noting is that you will need the additional ingredients listed below if you plan to make the delicious sushi and sashimi recipes in Part 2 of this book.

Fruits, Vegetables, and More

Always consider the various fruits and vegetables you plan on adding to your recipe. Ripe tropical fruits, for example, provide a delicious sweetness to your sushi, along with a colorful garnishment for a fanciful presentation. Don't forget the traditional garden vegetables you have around the kitchen, as well as specialty vegetables like enoki mushrooms, pickled ginger, or seaweed, which you will probably have to purchase especially for the occasion. Without question, fruits and vegetables create unique flavors that you and your guests will enjoy.

Tropical Fruits

Tropical fruits add color and sweetness to a variety of sushi items as well as making a fanciful garnish. Some of the popular fruits include: bananas, mangos, and papayas. Use these fruits (make sure they're ripe) as garnishment and in such rolls as the Tokyo Roll and the Tropical Roll.

Garden Vegetables

Similar to fruit, fresh vegetables add color, crunch, and excitement to a number of sushi dishes. The veggies you will likely use most are:

Cucumber (English or Japanese) The English variety works well, especially when slicing the cucumber to make the Cucumber Salad Roll. However, the Japanese cucumber is a great alternative. This long, slender cucumber has a thin, delicious skin, very little seeds, and doesn't hold much water so your rolls won't get waterlogged.

Cucumbers are a popular vegetable in sushi and will be used for such dishes as the popular California Roll, Caterpillar Roll, Cucumber Roll, Cucumber Salad Roll, Eel Roll, Futomaki Roll, Indian Roll, Local Roll, Montecito Roll, Moonlight Roll, Philadelphia Roll, Pink Paradise Roll, Rainbow Roll, Salmon Skin Roll, Shrimp Tempura Roll, Snake Roll, Spider Roll, Torpedo Roll, and Vegetable Roll, along with Hawaiian Poke, Salmon Skin Salad, and Spicy Jellyfish Salad.

Asparagus Asparagus is another vegetable finding its way into many sushi dishes. Since asparagus tends to be quite long, spears for sushi are often cut to about four inches in length—the perfect size to tuck inside a roll. Prepare asparagus by either steaming it or dipping it in tempura batter and deep-frying it for added crunch.

You'll find asparagus as an attractive ingredient in the Dragon Roll, Moonshine Roll, Pink Paradise Roll, Samurai Roll, Sun Rise Roll,

Stuffed Calamari Roll, Vegetable Crunchy Roll, and as an accompaniment to the Japanese Sea Bass dish.

Avocado Technically a fruit, the avocado rivals the cucumber for most appearances in sushi rolls and side dishes. Often sliced thin before being placed inside various rolls, the soft, creamy texture of the avocado is a nice compliment to the other, more firm, ingredients. You'll find avocado used in most rolls in Part 2.

Other Popular Veggies

Really, you and your guests decide what everyone likes and dislikes, and you can easily substitute fruits and vegetables for others, particularly when preparing the Vegetable Roll or the Vegetable Crunchy Roll.

Vegetables you might want to keep in the crisper and include in the recipes in Part 2 are: broccoli, cabbage, endive, jalapeño peppers, maui onions, shiitake mushrooms, tomatoes, and zucchini.

Japanese Specialty Vegetables

Now that you have purchased the necessary fruits and vegetables at your local supermarket, you might have to do a little digging for the Japanese staples that are a must when making sushi and sashimi. The Internet is a fantastic resource to shop online for the perishable essentials. If you live in an area that has an Asian or Japanese market, that is an even better place to shop.

The specialty items you will want to acquire are:

Daikon Radish Sprouts *(Kaiware)* These sprouts with their sharp, peppery taste are extremely popular in Japanese cuisine. You'll use these sprouts as garnish, in sauces like Chili Daikon, and tucked inside many of the sushi rolls in Part 2 of this book. Before using the sprouts, simply wash and pat them dry with a paper towel, then remove what you need with a sharp knife.

Enoki Mushrooms Also called velvet shanks or golden needle mushrooms, enoki are fruity in flavor with a crisp texture. They make an attractive and delicious garnish for the Japanese Sea Bass recipe in Part 2. When purchasing fresh enoki mushrooms, select those with firm, white, and shiny caps.

Pickled Gobo Root (a.k.a. Mountain Burdock or *Yamagobo*) This long, slender root resembles a skinny carrot. Buy them whole and often pickled and packed in sealed plastic. You'll use this crisp orange vegetable in such recipes as the Gobo Roll, Futomaki Roll, Salmon Skin Roll, Salmon Skin Salad, and the Vegetable Roll.

Food Corner

China continues to lead the world in ginger production with a global share of almost 25 percent followed by India, Nepal, and Indonesia.

Pickled Ginger *(Amazu Shoga* or *Gari)* A major player in the sushi world, pickled ginger can be found beside virtually every sushi dish and is an important garnishment. Not only does eating the tart ginger cleanse your palate and refresh your taste buds, but experts believe it also aids in destroying harmful parasites that may be present in raw fish.

Scallions (Green onions) Finely sliced is how you'll find scallions used in various sushi dishes. Not only do scallions make a colorful accoutrement, but their crisp mild taste also adds the perfect essence to sauces like Ponzu or makes a topping for halibut, monkfish liver, and shrimp sashimi.

Seaweed *(Wakame)* *Wakame* is a thin, stringy seaweed, deep green in color, and quite popular in such recipes as Hawaiian Poke, Ocean Salad Roll, and Salmon Skin Salad. While nori, the seaweed used for rolling sushi, is usually sold dried in sheets, you can find *wakame* either dried or fresh, in a refrigerated and sealed package. Whenever possible, buy fresh—it's much better tasting. If you have to settle for dry, add water to rehydrate the seaweed and bring it back to life.

Shiso Leaf *(Ooba)* Used as both a garnishment and active ingredient, shiso leaves are as attractive as they are delicious. Although they take on an herb-laden flavor similar to basil, shiso is actually from the mint family. When purchasing this aromatic leaf, look for fresh shiso leaves that are bright green in color.

Exotic Items

Three additional items you should store in the refrigerator prior to preparing sushi and sashimi are:

Quail Eggs Small and bite-size, fresh quail eggs add a splash of color and interest to such creations as the eyes in Big Eyes Sushi and the sun-yellow topping for salmon roe sushi, uni sushi, and the artistic uni shooter.

Tofu (Soybean Curd) This is one item you should be able to find at your local market as tofu is now known across the country. Tofu is sold in various packaging, from sealed in water to vacuum-packed. Like canned tuna, tofu packed in water is best and should be eaten right away. When it comes to texture, select the regular or firm tofu, which you will need for making the delectable sea bass dish in Part 2.

Tofu, Deep-Fried *(Abura Age)* Deep-fried tofu is a unique item with a sweet, moist texture. It is sold fresh in packages and serves as a delicious container for the rice in the Inari recipe.

Food Corner

Although the creation of tofu is not exactly known, legend has it that the first batch was created by accident. A cook was working with cooked soybeans when he produced a curd that we know today as tofu.

The Bottled and Dry Goods

Fortunately for home sushi chefs, a fair amount of ingredients do not need to be purchased fresh from the market because many of these items take the form of bottled liquids and dried goods.

So let's run down the list of bottled and dry ingredients you'll need for the recipes in Part 2. We'll divide these items between your local grocer and an Asian or Japanese specialty market. And do not worry about making an extra trip. More than likely you'll use these ingredients in other dishes you prepare, so it's a good idea to stock up and refer to your pantry when Japanese cuisine comes calling:

Cooked Squash *(Kanpyo)* *Kanpyo* is an ingredient used in traditional Japanese cuisine. You'll find it in the Futomaki Roll.

Dried Fish Flakes *(Katsuobushi)* These shavings from the bonita make an excellent topping for the Futomaki Roll and Salmon Skin Salad.

Dried Seaweed *(Nori)* An essential ingredient when crafting sushi rolls, nori is a layer of seaweed that has been dried and pressed into sheets. The best-tasting nori is dark green, and the size you should select is seven inches by eight inches although all recipes in this book call for cutting the sheet in half. If possible, purchase roasted nori, but if unavailable, simply roast the nori yourself by baking the sheet in a preheated 350°F oven for about one minute.

Dried Shiitake Mushrooms Fresh mushrooms are more desirable but not always in season. With dried shiitakes, simply soak them in cold water (not hot) to rehydrate prior to use. I feature shiitakes in the Futomaki Roll and Japanese Sea Bass recipes.

Flour Always have some all-purpose flour on hand. When it comes to tempura recipes, you'll be dusting most ingredients in flour before battering and deep-frying.

Hot Chili Sauce This bottled variety is an essential for any recipe that needs a kick, such as Shrimp Sushi or the savory Dragon Roll. Huy Fong Foods produces a tasty sauce.

Oil Like flour, oil will be an essential ingredient when deep-frying tempura-style. For searing seafood, such as tuna, try sesame oil for a distinctive flavor.

Ponzu Sauce Nothing beats the real thing, and I include the recipe in Part 2, but if you have to buy bottled, there are a few brands on the market.

Rice There is no such thing as Japanese cuisine without rice or sushi for that matter. To prepare premium, sticky rice with authentic taste and texture to use in various sushi and sushi rolls, always buy a high-quality Japanese short- or medium-grain white rice like koshihikari.

Food Corner

Traditionally, rice was eaten at every meal in Japan. Today, it is eaten plain and with sushi.

Rice Noodles The principal ingredients of these noodles are rice flour and water. I prefer these noodles when garnishing larger dishes, such as the Stuffed Calamari Roll or Tiger Eye.

Rice Vinegar This is the secret ingredient that gives prepared sushi rice its clean, crisp flavor. Mitsukan Gold makes a high-quality product.

Sake Sake is the celebrated Japanese alcoholic beverage made from rice. Always have a bottle of high-quality sake on hand for your sushi dinner parties. A tip worth noting: sake is often served warm or hot to disguise cheap sake, premium sake is always serve chilled.

Food Corner

Just as one needs a special kind of grape to produce a fine wine, making premium sake requires the use of a special type of rice. The secret is to have a variety of rice with a high starch content. This allows the rice to stay intact longer during the brewing process, enabling excess oil and protein to be removed.

Sesame Seeds Other than nori and sushi rice, this is probably the third most popular ingredient in sushi making, so buy plenty, preferably the toasted variety. In certain recipes, like the Spider Roll, I call for black sesame seeds because they are more attractive and nuttier in flavor.

Soybean Paper Some sushi rolls use soybean paper, a prettier and milder alternative to the traditional nori. Pressed from soybeans, these edible papers add dazzling color to such dishes as the Moonshine Roll and Pink Paradise Roll.

Soy Sauce Originating in China and introduced to Japan centuries ago, this sauce, made from soybeans, roasted grain, water, and salt, is a staple in sushi and sashimi dining. With more than half a dozen kinds on the market, stick with the regular or standard naturally-brewed soy sauce rather than other varieties. The Lite or with less salt is equally delicious.

Tempura Batter Mix Although you can make it from scratch, many Asian and Japanese markets carry quick and delicious batters in boxed form. Keep a few on hand, as various tempura foods are show-cased inside sushi rolls.

Wasabi Wasabi can be purchased raw or in a manufactured paste form (a combination of food coloring, horseradish, and mustard). Like pickled ginger, wasabi is often served with sushi or sashimi and often accompanies soy sauce. A dry, powdered form is also available, but the premade paste is much more convenient in today's kitchen.

Food Corner

Many wasabi powder and paste products available in supermarkets and even some restaurants contain very little or no real wasabi at all, but are made of colored horseradish instead because cultivation of real wasabi is relatively difficult and expensive.

Like selecting seafood, feel free to experiment with different fruits and vegetables to see what you like best. The same holds true with the bottled and dry ingredients as much of it tends to do with your personal taste, such as the color of sesame seeds or dry versus paste-form wasabi. We are giving you the guidelines; the rest is up to you.

The Least You Need to Know

- Common fruits and vegetables in sushi include banana, mango, and papaya, and asparagus, avocado, and cucumber.
- Visit an Asian or Japanese specialty market for those items not available at your local market.
- Stock up on the bottled and dry ingredients so you always have them on hand.

Chapter 3

The Sushi Kitchen

In This Chapter

- The essential tools
- Helpful kitchen gadgets
- Setting up your workspace

Once you have all of your ingredients, you will need to prepare the kitchen. In this chapter, you will discover the basic and easy-to-use tools needed to prepare sushi and sashimi recipes. Most of these tools are very specific to Japanese cuisine, such as a bamboo rolling mat and a high-quality sashimi knife. Besides the essential tools, we will also highlight some helpful kitchen gadgets that will make the preparation process much easier. Many of these items are common kitchen tools, such as a vegetable peeler, which is used frequently. The objective here is to provide you with an ideal model of how to set up your workspace for the tidiest and most efficient way to prepare your sushi or sashimi while staying organized.

Essential Tools

Sushi and sashimi is one cuisine that is not only delicious and healthy but also very easy to make. To do so, you'll need fresh ingredients, this book, and a handful of essential kitchen tools. Unlike other foods that may require expensive equipment, like a Cuisinart, pizza oven, or sorbet maker, you can purchase sushi utensils at relatively little cost, and they should last for a long time.

Let's discuss the right tools for the job.

Your Hands

Your hand is one of the most important tools for sushi making. Your fingers and palms will form the rice for all your sushi, and your finger tips will help craft the perfect sushi roll.

Forming sushi rice by hand.

James O. Fraioli

Making a sushi roll.

James O. Fraioli

Rolling a sushi roll.

James O. Fraioli

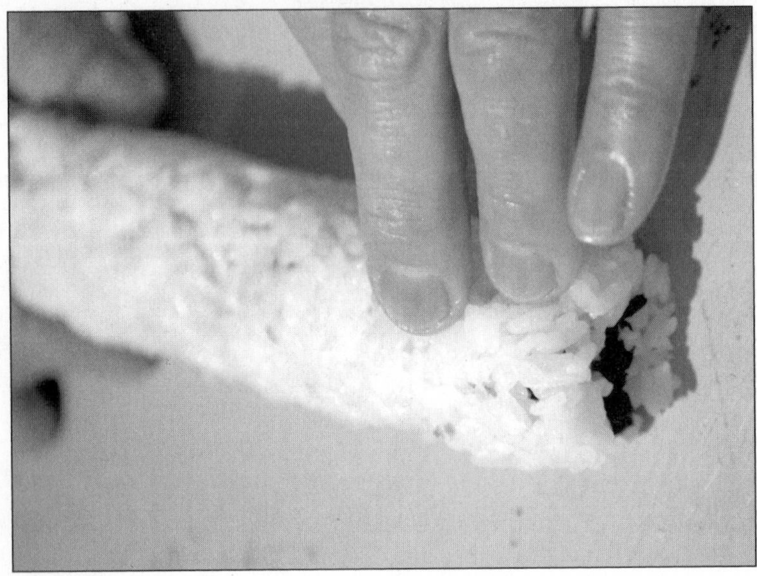

A completed sushi roll.

James O. Fraioli

Bamboo Sushi Mat

This inexpensive tool aids in making the sushi rolls and can be purchased at major kitchen stores or Asian and Japanese markets. The mat is comprised of strips of bamboo roughly nine inches square, but Chef Kaz Sato has removed the complexity of using this tool. In other words, he prefers to use his hands and fingers to roll the sushi and only uses the mat to compact the roll nice and tight before slicing and serving.

From the Kitchen

The Japanese have long believed that bamboo possesses mysterious powers and using bamboo in the kitchen will ward off harmful spirits. In Japan, bamboo symbolizes longevity, good health, and endurance since it remains green all year round and flourishes almost everywhere.

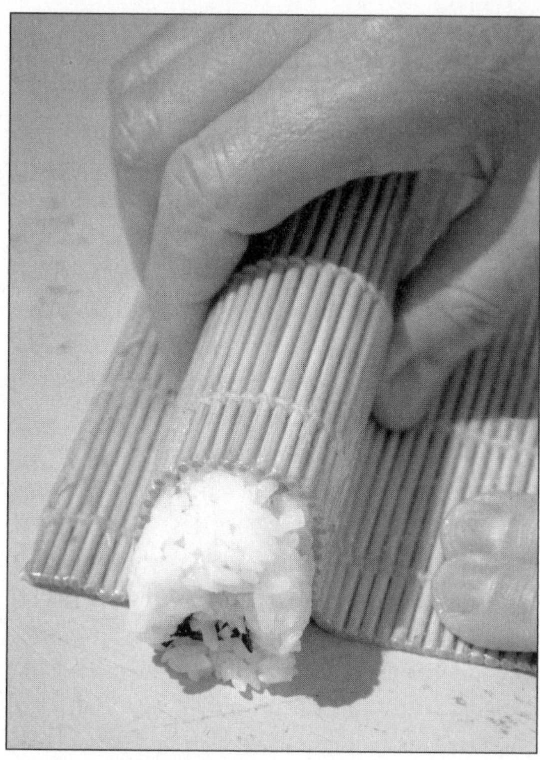

Compacting the sushi roll.

James O. Fraioli

Electric Rice Cooker

As you might expect, rice is an essential ingredient when making sushi. For superior results, your rice must be light and fluffy yet sticky. The conventional method of preparing sushi rice on the stove top is becoming a thing of the past as electric rice cookers prove to be much more efficient. Like blenders and coffee makers, rice cookers come in a bevy of makes and models. We suggest picking up a high-quality nonstick electric rice cooker that can hold 5 or 10 cups of rice, depending on how often you make sushi. As for the vital accessories you'll need to finish the rice, refer to Chapter 4.

From the Kitchen

Each rice cooker typically comes with a rice measuring cup which you should use for only that particular cooker. Often the graduations on the bowl for adding water rely on using that particular measuring cup. Since the rice cooker cups can vary in size, make a point to store both items together to avoid the guesswork later on.

Sashimi Knife *(Sashimi-hocho)*

A great variety of knives is on the market, and you can spend a lot of money collecting cleavers, filet knives, vegetable knives, you name it. But for simple-to-do sushi and sashimi at home, all you need is one or two high-quality Japanese knives. In fact, Chef Kaz Sato makes all the recipes in this book using just one knife. And that knife is a Sashimi Knife, aka *sashimi-hocho*, the Japanese equivalent to a western utility knife. This particular blade, ideal for everyday slicing and dicing, is also used for slicing fish, meats, and vegetables. The long carbon-steel blade (preferably eight inches) makes an excellent slicer and carving knife for long pieces of fish or vegetables. The razor-sharp blade also works well for creating garnishes, cutting sushi rolls, and filleting fish. Start with this blade, and add other knives later if necessary.

From the Kitchen

Unlike western knives, Japanese knives are often sharpened so only one side holds the cutting edge. Some Japanese knives are also angled from one or both sides. Since most people place a knife in their right hand, often it is only the right hand side of the blade that is angled. Left-handers must special order to receive their proper-fitting knife.

Helpful Kitchen Gadgets

Many of these suggested kitchen gadgets may be hiding in your drawers or cupboards at home, so now is the time to dust them off and get them ready. If you don't have these items, you might want to pick them up the next time you shop for groceries or household items.

Aluminum foil You need foil when cooking your fish or sushi in the toaster oven or under the broiler.

Bamboo skewers Use these when cooking your shrimp *(ebi)* so they don't curl when submerged in boiling water.

Bowl of water (or vinegar water) If you don't want your knife to stick when slicing your rolls, dip the blade in the bowl before you cut.

Chopsticks Although sushi is considered a finger food which can be eaten with your hands, many people dine with chopsticks. Pick up a pair and practice so you don't have to ask for a knife and fork the next time you eat sushi.

Cutting board Unless you enjoy hacking up your countertop, cutting boards provide an effective surface for all your slicing and dicing needs.

Kitchen towels Use these to clean, clean, clean. They also work well as an oven mitt in a pinch.

Measuring cups & spoons Measuring cups you'll use primarily for liquids. Measuring spoons are helpful when making the various sauces featured in Part 2.

Nonstick frying pans Nonstick eliminates the use of heavy nonstick sprays or butter and oils. You will need a high-quality pan when searing tuna or making scrambled egg for some of the sushi recipes.

Plastic wrap An important item for making your bamboo mat nonstick, it's also used when rolling your sushi roll in tempura crumbs and helps when slicing crumbed and fish-topped rolls so nothing sticks together.

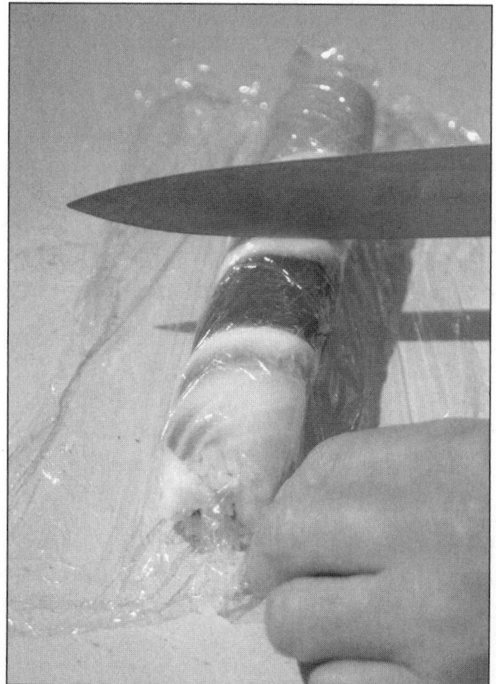

Slicing a sushi roll wrapped in plastic wrap.

James O. Fraioli

Toaster Oven I could move this item up to the essentials category as Chef Kaz Sato prefers this item over the conventional oven. It's convenient, takes little space on the kitchen counter, and cooks your freshwater eel *(unagi)* and sushi rolls in a jiffy.

Tweezers Small fish have small bones, and tweezers are the perfect tool for plucking them from a fresh fillet prior to consumption.

Vegetable Peeler Not all sushi recipes call for skin-on fruits and vegetables, so keep this handy for peeling a cucumber when making the Cucumber Salad Roll for example.

Setting Up Your Workspace

Now that you have all the proper equipment, it's time to arrange your workspace in the most efficient method possible, regardless of your kitchen layout or design.

In front of you place a cutting board, a knife, the bowl of water to dip your blade in, and a kitchen towel to wipe everything clean. This is the preparation step where you will chop, cut, and slice your ingredients.

When all the ingredients are ready, have your bamboo rolling mat and plastic wrap off to the corner, ready to use.

Nearby, plug in your toaster oven. If you are not using one, preheat your oven to broil if you intend to bake any of the cooked items.

On the stove, you should have a deep pot or pan, a bottle of cooking oil standing by, along with a pair of tongs and a paper-towel lined plate. You need these tools to deep-fry the tempura items. Also have a few shallow bowls ready for making the tempura batter.

Now plug in the electric rice cooker so it is ready to go.

When prepping your work station, keep it simple, and keep it clean. If you are not good at multi-tasking, now is the time to learn as you will be performing a number of duties, from cutting and cleaning, to dipping and cooking, rolling and slicing, and returning unused ingredients to the refrigerator, all the while keeping your knife clean and damp and your guests pleasantly entertained. All of this may sound like a lot of work, but remember: the goal of making this cuisine is to have fun while staying focused and organized—the traits of any successful sushi chef.

The Least You Need to Know

- The essential tools for making sushi and sashimi are your hands, a bamboo rolling mat, an electric rice cooker, and a sharp Japanese sashimi knife.
- Get your helpful kitchen gadgets ready, including a toaster oven.
- Multi-tasking is important when making sushi and sashimi.

Chapter 4

Tips and Techniques

In This Chapter

- Making perfect sushi rice
- The right tools for the job
- Slicing, dicing, and deboning

This chapter will give you some tips and tricks on how to prepare and present sushi or sashimi that you will be proud to serve, along with a few time saving ideas. By the time you are finished, you should be able to make traditional Japanese rice as well as debone and slice various fish. You will also learn how to use all of the equipment reviewed in the previous chapter. This may seem overwhelming so relax and take a deep breath. When you are done, your guests will have wide-eyes and eager mouths.

Making the Rice

The first—and most important—step in sushi making is preparing the rice. Unlike conventional rice, sushi rice must be light and fluffy yet sticky so you can shape and form it. To many home cooks, this is easier said than done, and dozens of recipes out there can get you even more confused. But don't panic. We will walk you step-by-step through perfecting the ideal rice.

Prepared sushi rice.

James O. Fraioli

Before we begin the cooking process, we need to gather the right tools for the job.

Essential Equipment for Making the Rice

To make the perfect traditional Japanese rice for your sushi, you will need to familiarize yourself with the necessary equipment. You will need an electric rice cooker, a Japanese *hangiri* (or wooden bowl), a large paddle or spatula, and a fan to cool the rice quickly.

Electric Rice Cooker

As cookers come in a variety of makes and models (see Chapter 3), we suggest a high-quality nonstick electric rice cooker that can hold five or more cups of rice.

Japanese *Hangiri*

Use this wooden sushi tub to cool your rice and remove any extra moisture after the rice is cooked. They come in different sizes, but for those beginning the sushi rice-making process, we recommend a tub with a diameter of 12 to 16 inches.

If your tub is new, break it in as you would a wooden salad bowl. Simply fill the tub with water, and let it stand overnight. The tub should also be good and wet prior to filling it with rice, which will avoid any rice sticking to the tub.

Large Paddle or Spatula

Get yourself an actual rice paddle or a large wooden spatula, preferably one that is flat and not too thick. You'll use this to scoop the rice from the electric cooker to the tub and to toss the rice as it cools.

Fan

The fan can take the form of a traditional Japanese *uchiwa*—a flat, nonfolding fan which has been a familiar part of daily life for Japan since ancient times—or an electric fan correctly positioned on the kitchen counter. Whether you want to manually fan or to simply press a speed on your electric fan, the goal here is to create a cool breeze over your rice as you fold with the wooden spoon. This will allow your rice to cool as quickly as possible, an important element in making the perfect sushi rice.

The Rice

One rule you cannot forget is this—use only Japanese rice for sushi making. Instant rice, converted rice, or brown rice will not work. In order to have the perfect, white, fluffy, yet sticky rice which is moist, whole, springy, and flavorful, get yourself a high-quality Japanese rice.

High-quality means that the rice must be a premium short- or medium-grain white rice, sold by the bag at grocery stores as well as Asian and Japanese markets. Often, the labels on the bag of rice will clearly read: Japanese Rice or Sushi Rice.

Time to Cook

Now that you have the proper equipment and your bag of premium Japanese rice, let's make that perfect sushi rice.

To make approximately 6 cups of sushi rice, you will need these ingredients:

3 cups Japanese sushi rice

3 1/4 cups water

1/4 cup rice wine vinegar

1 TB. sugar

1 tsp. salt

1 TB. dashi fish stock (optional)

We are using 3 cups of rice to make 6 cups of cooked rice because rice expands to nearly double in size after it absorbs the water. Remember this as you do not want to make more rice than you need.

Preparation Steps

1. **Rinse, Swirl, and Drain** Before the actual cooking process, rinse the rice to remove any impurities. Rinsing will also give your rice a beautiful, shiny appearance with delicious flavor.

   Either in the electric cooker's inner pot or in a large glass mixing bowl, add rice and cover with cold water. Gently swirl the rice with your hand for about 30 seconds, and discard the cloudy water. Continue this step four or five times until the water is almost clear.

2. **Soaking** To give your rice a brilliant white color, soak it for approximately 30 minutes by adding 3 or 4 cups of water to the rice. Set this aside as you prepare the sushi vinegar.

3. **Sushi Vinegar** Add vinegar, sugar, salt, and dashi (optional) in a small sauce pan. Heat over low heat, and stir until sugar and salt are dissolved. (Note: do not let the mixture boil). When dissolved, remove the pot from the heat, and let mixture cool while you cook the rice.
4. **Cooking the Rice** Plug in your electric rice cooker, and transfer the soaked rice into its inner pot. Since the cooker is made exclusively for this task, let it do the work.

   Important Rule: do not open the lid during the entire cooking process. The steam is what gives sushi rice it's light, fluffy quality, and opening the lid during cooking will allow the steam to escape.

   When the rice has finished cooking (approx. 20 minutes), let it rest for about 15 minutes.
5. **Adding the Sushi Vinegar** After the rice has rested for 15 minutes, transfer the rice to the *hangiri*, and pour the sushi vinegar over the rice. *Note:* do not use a metallic bowl in place of the wooden *hangiri* tub because metals will mar the delicate flavors of the rice.

   Using a cutting motion, fold the rice with your wooden paddle or spatula while fanning to cool the rice. Fanning also gives sushi rice its unique glossy look. If you use the traditional Japanese fan, fan with one hand and toss the rice with the other. Otherwise, position the electric fan over the rice while you toss. Keep tossing and cooling until the rice reaches room temperature, which could take up to 10 minutes.
6. **Ready to Use** Use the rice immediately as it will be shiny and sticky. However, if you cannot use the rice right away, simply cover the tub with a damp cloth, which will keep your rice from hardening.

Slicing, Dicing, and Deboning

Sushi and sashimi is one cuisine that can appear incredibly delicious or frighteningly unappetizing depending on how well you can slice and plate your various seafood.

As mentioned in Chapter 3, working with a high-quality Japanese sashimi knife is essential. Just as an electric rice cooker will help you achieve the ideal rice, the sashimi knife, when used properly, will elevate your culinary talents to new heights.

Since nothing in sushi and sashimi cuisine is hidden under sauces or buried beneath pastry shells, it is vital that all your slices and dices look tempting and mouthwatering on the plate. Try these tips and tricks to help you.

Slicing Seafood

When slicing seafood, the most important rule is to make the pieces the same size and the same thinness or thickness depending on what you are serving.

Many professional sushi chefs like Chef Kaz Sato prefer slicing the seafood at an angle, so also try to master this technique.

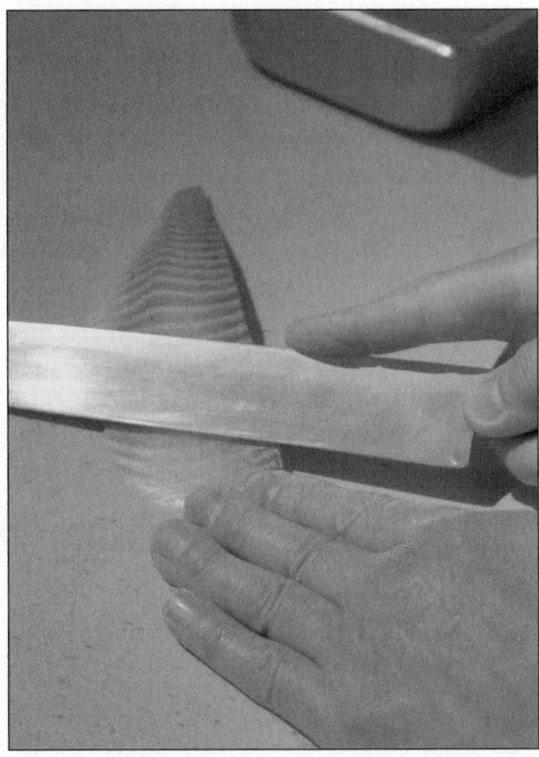

Slicing sashimi.

James O. Fraioli

Place the fresh fish loin or seafood on a cutting board in front of you. Dip your sashimi knife into a bowl of water so the blade is damp. This will avoid the knife sticking to the meat.

To slice at an angle, simply tilt the blade to the right so you are slicing diagonally across the piece of fish, also known as cutting against the grain. Start the knife away from you as you slice downward and to the left. Make the knife stroke one fluid motion, using the entire length of the blade until you finish the cut. Remember, you are not sawing; you are slicing. Continue these steps (along with dipping your knife in water after each cut) until you remove the amount of fish you need. This technique will apply to most types of seafood, not just fish filets or loins.

In general, slices for sushi will be thicker than sashimi, which is often sliced paper-thin.

Slicing sushi.

James O. Fraioli

For a paper-thin slice, which is how you should cut various white fish such as halibut and flounder, simply follow the steps for slicing seafood, but as the name implies, the slices should be almost transparent.

When plating sashimi, fan the paper-thin slices out on a plate accompanied by a colorful garnish, like pickled ginger and a pinch of wasabi.

Butterflying

Butterflying is a culinary term for cutting a particular piece of meat (shrimp, chicken, fish, etc.) so that it opens up like a book. This method is an excellent way to speed up the cooking time. For sushi and sashimi, it also serves as an attractive method for presenting the food.

To butterfly, place a shrimp, for example, on a cutting board in front of you. Place your fingers on top of the shrimp, carefully insert the knife into the thickest part of it, and draw the knife almost all the way through. Take care to keep the shrimp attached on one side.

Gently open the shrimp like a book and, if needed, use the broad side of the knife to even out the butterflied parts by lightly pounding the flesh until it's an even thickness.

How to Cut, Skin, Debone, and Fillet a Whole Fish

At some time you may purchase an entire fish to carve for sushi and sashimi, so here is a crash course on getting the whole fish ready for bite-size pieces.

Cutting

With a sharp knife, insert the blade behind the head while angling the knife toward the front of the fish. Slice down toward the bone, and continue downward just behind the fins to the stomach cavity.

Turn the fish, and run the knife just clear of the fins with a slight downward angle. When you feel the knife is down to the bone, reduce the angle and follow the bone until you come up against the backbone.

Peel the fillet back, and run the knife over the backbone, severing the small lateral fish bones in the process. Stop at this point. Turn the fish over, and repeat the first cut you made behind the fish head on the other side. Repeat the second cut near the dorsal fin with the knife angled slightly downward.

Continue this cut along the length of the fish. Reverse the direction of the filleting knife, and follow the bones by "feeling them" with the knife until you reach the backbone.

Peel the fillet back, and cut around the backbone and through the small lateral bones. Run the knife right through to the skin on the underside of the fish.

Cut over the belly flap either through or over the belly bones. Remove any remaining skin and then the first fillet. Flip the fish back to the original side, cut the bones around the stomach cavity, and release the remaining fillet from the backbone. There, your fish is filleted and ready for skinning and deboning.

Skinning

First, lay the fillet skin side down, and carefully cut between the fillet and skin while holding the knife at a shallow angle. This is the only cut where you move the knife back and forth. Stop when you have an inch or two of fillet released.

Change your grip on the fillet to a secure grip on the tab of fish skin you created with the first cut. Firmly hold the knife still and at a fixed angle. Wriggle the skin from side to side while pulling backward on the tab of fish skin. Continue this motion through the fillet until the skin is removed.

Deboning

You removed the backbones in the last filleting procedure, but bones remain around the stomach cavity, and a line of fine bones connect the backbone to the lateral line. The row of small bones which run vertically through the fillet are joined to the bones around the stomach cavity, and you can find them by inserting the knife at the front of the fillet.

Gentle strokes of a knife angled toward the stomach cavity will reveal the position of the fine bones. Follow this line, cutting completely through, to release the top part of the fillet.

The line of fine bones stops around two thirds of the way down the fillet. At this point, put the knife on the other side of the line of bones, and run the knife up the fillet until the point is well under the bones around the stomach cavity.

Separate the two, and reinsert the knife at an angle suitable to cut the flesh from the underside of the stomach bones, keeping the knife close to the bones to recover as much flesh as possible. Your fillet is now deboned.

Note: for any remaining loose bones, use a pair of tweezers to pluck the bones from the flesh.

The most important tip to remember is to arm yourself with the right kitchen tools for the job. And when investing in the proper equipment for making sushi and sashimi, do not scrimp on quality.

Working with Fruits and Vegetables

When preparing fruits and vegetables, particularly for the various sushi rolls featured in this book, the rule of thumb is to be consistent in your slices so each piece is even and uniform in both size and thickness.

The Japanese sashimi knife is an excellent blade for working with fruits and vegetables. If you find that the 8-inch blade is too long, you can downsize to a sashimi knife with a 6-inch blade.

Dicing

The secret to dicing fish or vegetables is that there is no secret. Dicing is simply cutting the particular food into small cubes. Just think slices, sticks, and then cubes. Let's use an example.

Say you want to dice a ripe mango for use in a recipe or as a garnish. First, place the mango on a cutting board; then peel, remove, and discard the skin.

Using your sashimi knife, slice two equal portions of mango, one on each side of the large pit, and discard the pitted section. Note: you may also want to remove the strips of mango on each side of the pit to reduce waste.

Cut each mango half lengthwise into even slices; then stack the slices and cut them into long sticks. Caution: mango can be quite slippery; so slice slowly and carefully, and watch your fingers at all times! Now cut the mango sticks crosswise into cubes, making the cubes as even as you can.

Dicing mango.

James O. Fraioli

This dicing technique will vary for specific fruits and vegetables, of course, but your goal should always be getting the fruits and vegetable into strips, which you can then easily cut into sticks and then cubes.

Vegetables made up of flowers, such as broccoli and cauliflower, are not typically diced, but broken into flowerets. The best, cleanest dice is made with a sharp knife; the sharper the better.

Cutting Corners

A number of kitchen gadgets on the market will slice, dice, and chop for you. Professional chefs prefer to use the knife, but for the home cook, convenience and less time spent in the kitchen often takes precedence.

If you prefer to set the knife aside when it comes to preparing fruits and vegetables, consider these helpful tools:

Chopper A small hand-operated tool with a sharp blade will uniformly chop various fruits and vegetables into small and large dices as long as you precut the items.

Mandoline This is a fancy word for a kitchen utensil consisting of two flat surfaces with a razor sharp blade mounted at a steep angle. A fruit or vegetable is pressed against the adjustable surface and moved into the blade and onto the fixed side so that a slice, which can be very thin, falls below the surfaces as it is cut.

The Least You Need to Know

- To make perfect sushi rice, you need an electric rice cooker, a Japanese *hangiri*, a large paddle or spatula, a fan, and premium Japanese rice.
- Get yourself a quality sashimi knife for slicing and dicing seafood, fruits, and vegetables.
- Cutting, filleting, skinning, and deboning a whole fish takes time and patience but is well worth the effort.

Part 2

The Recipes

Once you're comfortable with the basics, it's time to try the recipes in this part. From Sashimi à la Carte, to the more challenging sushi rolls, vegetarian options, and a collection of appetizers and salads your sushi dinner party is sure to be a hit.

Chapter 5

Sashimi à la Carte

In This Chapter

- Fifteen seafood delights
- Perfect dipping sauces
- Preparing and serving delicious sashimi

Castaway-Style Dining

You don't have to be marooned on a remote isle to appreciate raw fish today because there is an abundance of delectable choices fit for seafood lovers. But before we delve into the savory bounty, always remember the two important rules when preparing and serving sashimi: keep it fresh, and keep it simple. This allows the true essence of the fish to shine through.

When preparing fresh sashimi for your family or guests, serve only two pieces at a time, accompanied by an easy dipping sauce to enhance the flavor and an effortless garnish like daikon radish sprouts *(kaiware)*, pickled ginger, and a dab of wasabi paste. If you can do this, you have mastered the purest form of delicious ocean cuisine. Also you have no need to panic if some of your seafood is cooked. Not all sashimi is eaten raw. Items such as octopus and crab are always cooked prior to serving, otherwise you and your family and friends would be slurping the meal through a straw.

From the Kitchen

When trimming fish, precise measurements are not required. In fact, you can make sashimi just about any shape you like; the consistency and perfection sought in sushi restaurants is primarily for presentation.

Abalone (*Awabi*)

The meat of this mollusk in highly prized in the United States and Japan.

Serving size: 4 to 6 pieces	
Best Choice: Farm-raised abalone	**Preferred Dipping Sauce:** Soy sauce with wasabi

1. Remove abalone from shell and clean. With a sharp knife or scissors, remove black trim from meat. Next, slice abalone steak in half, lengthwise.
2. Angle the knife against one steak, and slice very thin portions (approximately 3-inches long by 1-inch wide) across the grain. Note: if pieces are cut too thick, meat will be too chewy to consume.
3. Transfer slices to a serving dish. Garnish with pinch of daikon radish sprouts (kaiware), pickled ginger, and dab of wasabi paste.

Food Corner

The correct way to flavor soy sauce with wasabi is to first place wasabi (paste form, never powder) into a small dish and then add soy sauce. This allows the wasabi to infuse the soy sauce much more subtly.

Albacore (*Shiro Maguro*)

The flavor of this fish is very rich but not overbearing.

Serving size: 4 to 6 pieces	
Best Choice: Troll-caught or pole-caught albacore	**Preferred Dipping Sauce:** Chili garlic sauce

1. Wash and dry fresh filet. Remove any skin or blood residue.
2. Sear filet on a hot grill for a few seconds on each side until entire outer edge turns opaque. Once complete, quickly place filet in an ice bath to immediately stop the cooking process. Remove filet, and pat dry with paper towel. Searing outside of filet ensures a moister fish.
3. With the knife blade at an angle, slice equal portions (approximately 3-inches long, 1-inch wide, and $^{1}/_{4}$-inch thick) across the grain.
4. Transfer slices to a serving dish. Garnish with pinch of daikon radish sprouts (kaiware), pickled ginger, and wasabi. Drizzle top with chili garlic sauce (Huy Fong Food makes a great bottled sauce) and sprinkle of sesame seeds.

Food Corner

Pickled ginger (*amazu shoga*) serves not only as a flavorful garnish but also helps kill harmful bacteria and parasites that may be present in raw seafood.

Baby Octopus *(Ii-dako)*

Baby octopus meat is very firm, slightly chewy, yet tender with a mild flavor. Octopus is usually sold whole fresh, frozen, or cooked, but you can also buy smoked and canned octopus. You can eat octopus raw, deep-fried, stewed, boiled, and pickled.

Serving size: 4 to 6 pieces	
Best Choice:	**Preferred Dipping Sauce:**
Frozen baby octopus	Soy sauce with wasabi

1. Defrost frozen octopus by soaking in cold water. Split in half, but do not sever completely.
2. Transfer octopus to a serving dish, and garnish with daikon radish sprouts (kaiware), thin carrot slices, and pinch of wasabi.

From the Kitchen

The edible parts of a baby octopus are the tentacles and body sac. To ready the octopus for eating, first remove the beak if it is present. The beak, actually the mouth, is found in the center of the tentacles. Also discard the eyes and the internal organs.

Cockle *(Torigai)*

The cockle has a wonderful taste and unique texture.

Serving size: 4 to 6 pieces	
Best Choice: Farmed or wild-caught cockles	**Preferred Dipping Sauce:** Soy sauce with wasabi

1. If fresh, remove meat from shell by severing small abductor muscles (which hold shell together) and scoop out flesh. If cockles are pre-cooked, wash, clean, and pat dry with a paper towel.
2. With the knife blade at an angle, slice cockle into equal portions.
3. Transfer cockle slices to a serving dish. Garnish with pickled ginger and pinch of wasabi.

Fish Facts

Today, farmed clams account for 89 percent of the world clam consumption. The majority of these clams consumed in the United States are farmed here, with most imports coming from Canada.

Fresh Water Eel *(Unagi)*

There's nothing "fishy" about eels; they are well-cooked and a favorite for many who shy away from raw fish.

Serving size: 4 to 6 pieces	
Best Choice:	**Preferred Dipping Sauce:**
Farmed or wild Japanese eel	Eel sauce (recipe in Chapter 7)

1. With the knife blade at an angle, slice equal portions (approximately 3-inches long, 1-inch wide, and 1/4-inch thick) across the grain. Do not remove skin.
2. Transfer slices to a serving dish, skin side down. Garnish with pickled ginger and drizzle of eel sauce.

Food Corner

Most fresh water eel served in the United States has been bought processed, cooked, frozen, and shipped in sealed packets for convenience.

Halibut *(Hirame)*

Hirame is the most popular of the white-meat sushi fish.

Serving size: 4 to 6 pieces	
Best Choice: Pacific halibut	**Preferred Dipping Sauce:** Soy sauce with wasabi

1. With the knife blade at an angle, slice across the grain very thin portions (approximately 3-inches long, 1-inch wide). Each piece should look almost transparent.
2. Remove any skin.
3. Transfer slices to a serving dish. Garnish top of each slice with fresh ginger, pinch of finely chopped scallions (green onions), drizzle of olive oil and soy sauce, and sprinkle of sesame seeds; place pinch of wasabi alongside.

Food Corner

Not only is halibut low in calories and cholesterol, but it is also very easy to digest. Halibut meat contains collagen which is responsible for healthy, young-looking skin.

King Crab *(Kani)*

King crab is prized for its immense sweet meat, which is always cleaned and cooked prior to reaching the market.

Serving size: 4 to 6 pieces	
Best Choice: Alaskan king crab	**Preferred Dipping Sauce:** Soy sauce

1. Crack shell of one or two king crab legs and carefully remove meat so piece remains intact.
2. Wipe away any residue, formed during the cooking process, and with a sharp knife blade at an angle, slice equal portions (approximately 3-inches long, 1-inch wide, and 1/4-inch thick) across the grain.
3. Transfer slices to a serving dish. Garnish with green shiso leaf (ooba).

Fish Facts

Three species of king crab live in Alaska—red, blue, and brown. The true red king crab is the most prized species of crab in the world.

Mackerel *(Saba)*

The flavor of mackerel can be a little fishy and oily but pleasant-tasting overall.

Serving size: 4 to 6 pieces	
Best Choice: Horse, King, or Spanish mackerel (Aji)	**Preferred Dipping Sauce:** Ponzu sauce (recipe in Chapter 7)

1. If buying whole, remove head and entrails. Clean thoroughly and pat dry with paper towel.
2. Slice mackerel in half, lengthwise.
3. Remove bones, particularly along the spine. (Note: a large pair of tweezers works well to pluck the bones from the flesh).
4. Remove skin and any blood residue.
5. With the knife blade at an angle, slice equal portions (approximately 3-inches long, 1-inch wide, and 1/4-inch thick) across the grain. Next, score top of each piece with a knife, creating a crosshatch pattern.
6. Transfer mackerel slices to a serving dish. Garnish top of each slice with fresh ginger and pinch of finely chopped scallions. Drizzle with ponzu sauce, and sprinkle with sesame seeds. Place pinch of wasabi alongside.

Food Corner

Because mackerel meat can spoil quickly, it is the only common salt-cured sushi/sashimi.

Octopus *(Tako)*

Octopus tentacles are often available precooked and lightly marinated. Keep in mind that fresh tentacles should be pleasantly chewy while old tentacles will appear tough to the pallet.

Serving size: 4 to 6 pieces	
Best Choice:	**Preferred Dipping Sauce:**
Hawaiian octopus	Soy sauce with wasabi

1. With the knife blade at an angle, slice very thin portions (approximately 3-inches long, 1-inch wide, and 1/4-inch thick) across the grain of one octopus arm. (Note: if slices are cut too thick, octopus will be too chewy).
2. Transfer slices to a serving dish, and garnish with fresh lemon slices.

From the Kitchen

Sliced octopus tentacles are perfect for sashimi while the tentacle end pieces are ideal for sushi rolls.

Salmon *(Sake)*

Larger salmon are generally used for sashimi due to their higher fat/oil content.

Serving size: 4 to 6 pieces	
Best Choice: Wild-caught salmon (Chinook, Coho, or Sockeye)	**Preferred Dipping Sauce:** Soy sauce with wasabi

1. Remove any skin, bones, or blood residue from salmon filet.
2. With the knife blade at an angle, slice equal portions (approximately 3-inches long, 1-inch wide, and 1/4-inch thick) across the grain.
3. Transfer slices to a serving dish, and garnish with pickled ginger and pinch of wasabi.

Fish Facts

The largest salmon is the Pacific King, also known as the Chinook The largest on record is a whopping 126 pounds, which was caught in Alaska.

Sea Bream *(Tai)*

Although often farm-raised, bream from the ocean tends to have the better flavor compared to the farmed freshwater variety.

Serving size: 4 to 6 pieces	
Best Choice: Wild caught ocean bream	**Preferred Dipping Sauce:** Soy sauce with wasabi

1. If buying whole bream, remove head and entrails. Clean thoroughly, and pat dry with paper towel.
2. Slice fish in half, lengthwise.
3. Remove bones, particularly along spine. (Note: a large pair of tweezers works well to pluck bones from flesh).
4. Remove skin and any blood residue.
5. With the knife blade at an angle, slice equal portions (approximately 3-inches long, 1-inch wide, and 1/4-inch thick) across the grain.
6. Transfer slices to a serving dish. Garnish with pickled ginger and pinch of wasabi.

Fish Facts

In the United States, **tai** can also refer to Red Snapper, which is a common delicacy throughout Japan.

Shrimp *(Ebi)*

Ebi is often purchased at the market with whitish pink and slightly steamed flesh. Raw *ebi* is equally delicious.

Serving size: 4 to 6 pieces	
Best Choice: Pink shrimp and spot prawns	**Preferred Dipping Sauce:** Ponzu sauce (recipe in Chapter 7)

1. If purchasing whole shrimp, remove tail section and discard shell. Wash under cold water, and remove black vein that runs along spine. Damp dry with a paper towel.
2. With a sharp knife, butterfly tail sections so each shrimp lies flat. Do not sever tail entirely.
3. Transfer slices to a serving dish. Place pinch of chili daikon (equal parts of finely chopped daikon radish sprouts and bottled hot chili sauce) on top of each piece, along with finely chopped scallion. Drizzle with ponzu sauce and squeeze of lemon.

Food Corner

Shrimp are often divided and sold in three categories based upon their habitat: coldwater or northern; warm-water, tropical or southern; and freshwater.

Tuna *(Maguro)*

The big-eye tuna, sometimes called *ahi*, is far better tasting than *ahi* and is often served as *maguro.*

Serving size: 4 to 6 pieces	
Best Choice: Big-eye tuna	**Preferred Dipping Sauce:** Soy sauce with wasabi

1. With the knife blade at an angle, slice equal portions (approximately 3-inches long, 1-inch wide, and 1/4-inch thick) across the grain.
2. Remove any skin or blood residue.
3. Transfer slices to a serving dish. Garnish with pickled ginger and pinch of wasabi.

Food Corner

The best "sushi-grade" is bluefin tuna meat; unfortunately the high demand has taken its toll. Today, bluefin tuna is severely overfished in all oceans. In the United States, some sushi bars are now substituting big-eye tuna for bluefin, which is equally as tasty.

Tuna Belly *(Toro)*

Toro commands the highest price because of the tuna belly's delectable fat content.

Serving size: 4 to 6 pieces	
Best Choice:	**Preferred Dipping Sauce:**
Big-eye tuna	Soy sauce with wasabi

1. With the knife blade at an angle, slice equal portions (approximately 3-inches long, 1-inch wide, and 1/4-inch thick) across the grain.
2. Remove any skin or blood residue.
3. Transfer slices to a serving dish, and garnish with pickled ginger and pinch of wasabi.

Food Corner

Shop carefully. Sometimes cuts of tuna labeled toro, come from a section of the fish where connective tissue (suji) runs through most of the tender meat. This lower-grade cut is very tough to chew, and should not be purchased.

Yellowtail *(Hamachi)*

Don't let the color of yellowtail fool you. The flesh is often pinkish-brown in the United States, while silver in Japan. Both varieties are equally delicious.

Serving size: 4 to 6 pieces	
Best Choice: Farm-raised or wild-caught yellowtail amberjack	**Preferred Dipping Sauce:** Ponzu sauce (recipe in Chapter 7)

1. With the knife blade at an angle, slice equal portions (approximately 3-inches long, 1-inch wide, and 1/4-inch thick) across the grain.
2. Remove any skin or blood residue.
3. Transfer slices to a serving dish. Place few paper-thin slices of jalapeño pepper on top of each slice. Garnish with pickled ginger, pinch of wasabi, and drizzle of ponzu sauce. Sprinkle with sesame seeds.

Food Corner

Yellowtail is a sushi and sashimi staple. In Japan, at least three other names are used for yellowtail, depending on its maturity and color: *Buri*, *Kanpachi*, and *Inada*.

Chapter 6

Sushi

In This Chapter

- Twenty-five seafood delights
- Delicious dipping sauces
- Secret sushi tricks

This chapter showcases 25 delightful sushi recipes and the best choices of seafood that will provide the most flavors for your sushi. This is important, especially when making that trip to the grocery store. The accompanying recipes to follow are fun and easy to make whether for yourself or for a group of people. And, of course, no recipe can be complete without the proper dipping sauce, such as the familiar soy sauce with wasabi. Plenty of recommendations will assist you along the way so you can prepare mouth-watering treats for everyone to appreciate.

As with any raw food, when you eat sushi, you risk food-borne illnesses caused by bacteria, parasites, and toxins.

Big Eyes Sushi

This sushi creation is a fun way to present fresh fish with an artistic flare.

Serving size: 2 pieces

Best Choice: Pacific halibut and wild-caught salmon

Preferred Dipping Sauce: Eel sauce (recipe in Chapter 7)

½ sheet *nori*

4 TB. prepared sushi rice

2 pieces halibut (approximately 1-inch wide by 3- or 4-inches long)

2 pieces salmon (approximately 1-inch wide by 3- or 4-inches long)

2 TB. spicy sauce (recipe in Chapter 7)

2 slices avocado

2 TB. crab mixture (recipe in Chapter 7)

2 quail eggs

Eel sauce, to taste (recipe in Chapter 7)

Scallion (green onion), finely chopped

Sesame seeds, as needed

1. With scissors, cut two thick strips from sheet, nori, each 1½- to 2-inches wide by about 4-inches long.
2. Roll strips with your fingers, creating two collars.
3. Fill each collar ½ full with rice.
4. With a sharp damp knife blade at an angle, slice two thin portions of fresh halibut across the grain. Wrap one slice of halibut around one side of outer seaweed of each collar. Cover remaining sides with pieces of fresh salmon, sliced in the same manner as the halibut.
5. Fill each container above rice with spicy sauce, leaving ¼ room on top.
6. Slice two pieces of avocado, and wrap around each upper lip of seaweed collars, above halibut and salmon.
7. Fill each collar with 1 TB. fresh crabmeat mixture. Form small crater with a teaspoon.

8. Inside each crater, add quail egg so yolk rests in center.
9. Transfer containers to a baking sheet lined with foil, and place in a toaster oven or under the broiler until eggs are poached. This takes several minutes; watch carefully.
10. Remove containers, transfer to a serving dish, and garnish with drizzle of eel sauce, pinch of finely chopped scallion, and sprinkle of sesame seeds.

Food Corner

The best tasting *nori* is dark green to almost black in color. Red or brown *nori* is typically old and poor tasting.

Conch *(Horagai)*

All parts of conch meat are edible. However, most people find the firm white meat the only appetizing section. If purchasing fresh conch, often the meat has already been removed from the shell. Conch meat may also be precooked. Both varieties are equally suitable for sushi.

2 pieces horse or queen conch

Wasabi, to taste

4 TB. prepared sushi rice

½ sheet *nori*

Pickled ginger

Serving size: 2 pieces

Best Choice: Horse or Queen Conch

Preferred Dipping Sauce: Soy sauce with wasabi

1. With a sharp knife placed at an angle, slice conch in two very thin portions approximately 3-inches long, 1-inch wide across the grain.
2. Using your fingertip, dab once or twice in wasabi and smear on both pieces of conch.
3. Dip hands in water and scoop about 2 TB. prepared sushi rice with your fingers. In your palm, form rice to conch pieces or a rectangular shape approximately 1-inch wide and 2-inches long. Repeat.
4. Place two pieces conch, wasabi side down, on rice.
5. For decoration and to help secure conch to rice, cut two narrow strips from nori with scissors. Each strip should be about ¼-inch wide by about 4-inches long. Wrap each strip around conch and rice.
6. Transfer two conch pieces to a small serving dish. Garnish with pickled ginger and pinch of wasabi.

Food Corner

When buying conch, ask where it comes from. Both the commercial and recreational conch fisheries in Florida are closed due to overfishing, and only a few conch-exporting nations have adequate management and stocks that are not yet overfished.

Egg Sushi *(Tamago)*

This simple recipe is also endearingly known as a sushi omelet.

Serving size: 2 pieces

1 egg

Pinch salt

Pinch sugar

4 TB. prepared sushi rice

1/2 sheet *nori*

1. To make two pieces of egg approximately 1/2-inch wide and 4-inches long, crack egg and whisk in a bowl. Add pinch of salt and pinch of sugar for sweetness. Pour into a nonstick fry pan over medium heat and scramble. Remove from heat and let cool. When cool, form eggs with your fingers to create strips. Set aside.
2. Dip your hands in water, and scoop about 2 TB. sushi rice with your fingers. In your palm, form rice to size of egg pieces or a rectangular shape approximately 1-inch wide and 2-inches long. Repeat.
3. For decoration and to help secure egg to rice, cut two narrow strips from nori with scissors. Each strip should be about 1/4-inch wide by about 4-inches long. Wrap each strip around egg and rice.
4. Transfer egg pieces to a small serving dish.

Flounder *(Hirame)*

Hirame, the name used for both halibut and flounder, is the most popular of the white-meat sushi fish.

2 pieces Pacific flounder

Wasabi, to taste

4 TB. prepare sushi rice

Fresh ginger, as needed

Scallions, finely chopped

Olive oil, as needed

Soy sauce, as needed

Sesame seeds, as needed

Serving size: 2 pieces

Best Choice: Pacific flounder

Preferred Dipping Sauce: Soy sauce with wasabi

1. With the knife blade at an angle, slice across the grain of flounder two very thin portions approximately 3-inches long and 1-inch wide. Each piece should look almost transparent. Remove any skin.
2. Using your fingertip, dab your finger in wasabi once or twice and smear on both pieces of flounder.
3. Dip your hands in water, and scoop about 2 TB. rice with your fingers. In your palm, form rice to size of flounder pieces or a rectangular shape approximately 1-inch wide and 2-inches long. Repeat.
4. Place flounder, wasabi side down, on rice.
5. Transfer flounder slices to a small serving dish. Garnish top of each slice with fresh ginger, pinch of scallions, drizzle of olive oil and soy sauce, sprinkle of sesame seeds, and pinch of wasabi alongside.

Food Corner

Pacific flounder is often a marketing name used for English Sole, Dover Sole, Petrale Sole, and Sanddab.

Lobster *(Ebi)*

Like crab, lobster meat is always precooked prior to consumption. If purchasing live lobster or raw lobster tails, boil them first in salted water.

2 pieces lobster tail

Wasabi, to taste

4 TB. prepared sushi rice

½ sheet *nori*

2 green shiso leaves

Serving size: 2 pieces

Best Choice: Maine lobster from the United States and Canada or spiny lobster from the United States, Baja, and Australia.

Preferred Dipping Sauce: Soy sauce with wasabi

1. Carefully remove cooked lobster meat from shell. Place under cold running water to clean any residue from the cooking process. Damp dry with a paper towel.
2. With a sharp knife placed at an angle, slice two thin portions approximately 3-inches long, 1-inch wide across the grain of lobster tail.
3. Dab your finger in wasabi once or twice, and smear on lobster.
4. Dip your hands in water, and scoop about 2 TB. rice with your fingers. In your palm, form rice to size of lobster or a rectangular shape approximately 1-inch wide and 2-inches long. Repeat.
5. Place lobster, wasabi side down, on rice.
6. For decoration and to help secure lobster to rice, cut two narrow strips about ¼-inch wide by about 4-inches long from nori with scissors. Wrap each strip around lobster and rice.
7. Transfer lobster pieces to a small serving dish. Garnish with green shiso leaf and pinch of wasabi.

Fish Facts

Long ago, Native Americans fertilized their fields with lobster and used them to bait their hooks in hopes of catching something more worth eating. During colonial times, lobster was considered "poverty food" and was harvested from tidal pools to serve to children, servants, and prisoners.

Monkfish Liver *(Ankimo)*

Ankimo, which looks like pâté, is a Japanese delicacy, often steamed or sautéed.

Prepackaged monkfish liver

Wasabi, to taste

4 TB. prepared sushi rice

$\frac{1}{2}$ strip *nori*

Chili daikon, as needed

Scallions, finely chopped, as needed

Ponzu sauce, as needed (recipe in Chapter 7)

Serving size: 2 pieces

Best Choice: Prepackaged monkfish liver

Preferred Dipping Sauce: Ponzu sauce (recipe in Chapter 7)

1. Slice two pieces approximately $\frac{1}{4}$-inch thick from tube of liver.
2. Using your fingertip, dab your finger in wasabi once or twice and smear both pieces of monkfish liver.
3. Dip your hands in water, and scoop about 2 TB. rice with your fingers. In your palm, form rice to size of liver pieces or a rectangular shape approximately 1-inch wide and 2-inches long. Repeat.
4. Place liver, wasabi side down, on rice.
5. For decoration and to help secure liver to rice, cut two narrow strips about $\frac{1}{4}$-inch wide by about 4-inches long from nori with scissors. Wrap each strip around liver and rice.
6. Transfer liver pieces to a small serving dish. Top each piece with chili daikon, pinch of scallions, and drizzle of ponzu sauce.

Food Corner

Monkfish liver comes from the monkfish, which is often sold fresh or frozen under the name goosefish. They are also known as anglerfish, angler, molligut, bellyfish, lawyerfish, and fishing frog. Caution: monkfish populations off the coast of the United States are in poor decline due to overfishing.

Salmon Popper

The Salmon Popper adds excitement to the sushi menu by offsetting the cool, rich texture of the salmon with the heat and crunchiness of the tempura jalapeño.

2 pieces salmon

Wasabi, to taste

4 TB. prepared sushi rice

1 Tempura jalapeño pepper

1/2 sheet *nori*

Serving size: 2 pieces

Best Choice: Wild-caught salmon (Chinook, Coho, or Sockeye)

Preferred Dipping Sauce: Soy sauce with wasabi

1. With the knife blade at an angle, slice two equal portions salmon approximately 3-inches long, 1-inch wide, and 1/4-inch thick across the grain.
2. Using your fingertip, dab your finger in wasabi once or twice, and smear on salmon.
3. Dip your hands in water, and scoop about 2 TB. rice with your fingers. In your palm, form rice to size of salmon or a rectangular shape approximately 1-inch wide and 2-inches long. Repeat.
4. Place two pieces of salmon, wasabi side down, on rice.
5. On top of salmon, add 1/4 tempura jalapeño.
6. For decoration and to help secure jalapeño and salmon to rice, cut two wide strips of nori with scissors. Each strip should be about 1-inch wide by about 5- or 6-inches long. Wrap each strip around jalapeño, salmon, and rice. With a knife, cut each piece in half.

From the Kitchen

To make tempura jalapeño: dust pepper in flour and shake off excess. Roll pepper in tempura batter (prepare according to package directions), and deep fry in hot oil until golden brown. Remove pepper, pat dry with paper towel, and cool. When cool, cut pepper in half lengthwise.

7. Transfer four tempura jalapeño/salmon pieces to a small serving dish.

From the Kitchen

To turn down the heat in a jalapeño pepper, remove the seeds. Capsaicin—the substance inside peppers which creates the hotness—is distributed into the seeds, and cooking will not reduce the heat if the seeds are not removed.

Scallop *(Hotategai)*

To highlight a scallop's slightly nutty flavor, always serve fresh, whole scallops.

2 scallops

Wasabi, to taste

4 TB. prepared sushi rice

½ sheet *nori*

Lemon peel, thinly slivered, as needed

Green shiso leaf, as needed

Serving size: 2 scallops

Best Choice: Farmed scallops or wild-caught sea scallops from the Northeast United States and Canada.

Preferred Dipping Sauce: Soy sauce with wasabi

1. With a sharp knife, butterfly each scallop by slicing lengthwise so scallop lies flat. Do not sever scallop completely.
2. Using your fingertip, dab your finger in wasabi, and smear on both pieces of scallop.
3. Dip your hands in water, and scoop about 2 TB. rice with your fingers. In your palm, form rice to scallop pieces or a rectangular shape approximately 1-inch wide and 2-inches long. Repeat.
4. Place two butter-flied pieces of scallop, wasabi side down, on rice.
5. For decoration and to help secure scallop to rice, cut two narrow strips from nori with scissors. Each strip should be about ¼-inch wide by about 4-inches long. Wrap each strip around scallop and rice.
6. Transfer scallop pieces to a small serving dish. Top with lemon peel, and garnish with green shiso leaf.

Food Corner

As a rule of thumb, farmed scallops are available year-round while wild-caught scallops are often limited in specific regions for food safety reasons.

Sea Eel *(Anago)*

The difference between sea eel *(anago)* and freshwater eel *(unagi)* is that sea eel is lighter in color with less fat and has a much more delicate flavor and texture.

2 pieces conger eel

Wasabi, to taste

4 TB. prepared sushi rice

Eel sauce, as needed (recipe in Chapter 7)

Sesame seeds, as needed

Serving size: 2 pieces

Best Choice: Conger Eel

Preferred Dipping Sauce: Eel sauce (recipe in Chapter 7)

1. Since sea eel is sold prepackaged and precooked and/or smoked, double-check the product. Remove any leftover fin fragments, which can be overlooked during processing.
2. With the knife blade at an angle, slice two large portions approximately 5-inches long, and 1- or 2-inches wide across the grain.
3. Place pieces of eel on a baking sheet lined with foil and place in a toaster oven or under the broiler until well heated.
4. Using your fingertip, dab your finger once or twice in wasabi, and smear on skin side of both pieces of eel.
5. Dip your hands in water, and scoop about 2 TB. rice with your fingers. In your palm, form rice to 1/2 size of eel piece or a rectangular shape approximately 1-inch wide and 2-inches long. Repeat.
6. Place eel pieces, wasabi and skin side down, on rice.
7. Transfer eel to a serving dish, and top with a drizzle of eel sauce and a sprinkle of sesame seeds.

Food Corner

While freshwater eel *(unagi)* is more common in United States sushi bars, sea eel *(anago)* is the eel of choice in Japan.

Sea Urchin *(Uni)*

The very best uni is fresh, creamy, sweet, and has a mild nutty or custardlike flavor.

½ sheet *nori*

4 TB. prepared sushi rice

2 pieces fresh uni

2 fresh quail eggs (if desired)

Soy sauce, as needed

Serving size: 2 pieces

Best Choice: Red sea urchin from Pacific United States waters

Preferred Dipping Sauce: Soy sauce

1. With scissors, cut two wide strips from nori, each 1½- to 2-inches wide by about 4-inches long.
2. Roll strips with your fingers, creating two collars.
3. Fill each collar ½ way with rice.
4. Spoon fresh uni on top of rice, filling collars.
5. Crack quail egg and place on uni (if desired).
6. Transfer uni to a small serving dish, and top with soy sauce.

Fish Facts

Inside a shell of the sea urchin is the *uni*—actually the urchin's gonads—which appear as five yellow-orange strips arranged in a star-shape pattern.

Shrimp Heads

Although the name doesn't sound very appetizing, this dish is quite delicious with its sweet, crunchy texture.

2 large shrimp or prawns

Corn starch, as needed

2 fresh green shiso leaves

2 slices lemon

Serving size: 2 pieces

Best Choice: Pink shrimp and spot prawns

Preferred Dipping Sauce: Soy sauce with wasabi

1. Purchase two large shrimp or prawns, and remove tail section, separating head, antenna, legs, and upper body as one piece. Reserve tail meat for sashimi or sushi.
2. Dust two pieces in corn starch, and deep fry in hot oil until shrimp turn a bright pink/red color. Carefully remove, and drain on paper towel.
3. Transfer shrimp to a serving dish, and garnish with shiso leaf and lemon slice.

Snow Crab *(Kani)*

Snow crab is noted for its sweet, delicate flavor, snow-white meat, and tender texture.

2 pieces snow crab

Wasabi, to taste

4 TB. prepared sushi rice

½ sheet *nori*

2 green shiso leaves

Serving size: 2 pieces

Best Choice: Wild-caught snow crab from Alaska or Canadian waters

Preferred Dipping Sauce: Soy sauce

1. Crack shell of one or two crab legs, and carefully remove meat so pieces remain intact.
2. Wipe away any residue formed during the cooking process, and with the knife blade at an angle, slice two equal portions approximately 3-inches long, 1-inch wide, and ¼-inch thick across the grain.
3. Using your fingertip, dab your finger one or twice in wasabi, and smear on both pieces of crab.
4. Dip your hands in water, and scoop about 2 TB. rice with your fingers. In your palm, form rice to size of crab pieces or a rectangular shape approximately 1-inch wide and 2-inches long. Repeat.
5. Place crab pieces, wasabi side down, on rice.
6. For decoration and to help secure crab to rice, cut two narrow strips of nori with scissors, each about ¼-inch wide by about 4-inches long. Wrap each strip around crab and rice.
7. Transfer crab pieces to a small serving dish, and garnish with shiso leaves.

Food Corner

The common market name "snow crab" is used not only for the true snow crab but also for the three species of tanner crab.

Squid *(Ika)*

Fresh squid should always look translucent and feel "fuzzy" on the tongue. The shinier the meat, often the older and tougher it is.

1 large squid

1 green shiso leaf

1 cucumber spear, approximately 3-inches long with skin

Lemon slices

Serving size: 4 to 5 pieces

Best Choice: Trawl-caught longfin (common) squid from the United States Atlantic Ocean.

Preferred Dipping Sauce: Soy sauce with wasabi

1. From a large squid, remove tail section, and split open with a knife creating a sheet of squid meat approximately 3-inches by 3-inches. If frozen, thaw in cold water, and pat dry with paper towel.
2. Place green shiso leaf and cucumber spear on squid.
3. Using your fingers, carefully roll squid meat around leaf and cucumber, forming a tight roll.
4. With a sharp, damp knife, slice in 4 to 5 pieces, and transfer to a small serving dish. Garnish with shiso leaf and slices of lemon.

Food Corner

Longfin squid is available fresh and frozen year-round. Shortfin squid is also available frozen most of the year but is only available fresh in the summer and fall.

Surf Clam *(Hokkigai)*

Like most clams in the sushi bar, *hokkigai* is rarely served raw.

2 pieces surf clams

Wasabi, to taste

4 TB. prepared sushi rice

Pickled ginger, to taste

Serving size: 2 pieces

Best Choice: Atlantic surf clams

Preferred Dipping Sauce: Soy sauce with wasabi

1. If surf clam is purchased, often meat has been removed from shell and precooked. Before preparing, split open each clam section with a sharp knife, and remove any remaining viscera. Wash under cold water, and pat dry with a paper towel.
2. Using your fingertip, dab in wasabi once or twice, and smear on clam pieces.
3. Dip your hands in water, and scoop about 2 TB. rice with your fingers. In your palm, form rice to size of clam pieces or a rectangular shape approximately 1-inch wide and 2-inches long. Repeat.
4. Place clam, wasabi side down, on rice.
5. Transfer clam pieces to a small serving dish, and garnish with pickled ginger and pinch of wasabi.

Food Corner

Also called "hen clam," surf clam looks like a cockle, white with a dark red tip, and is slightly crunchy. Atlantic surf clams are generally not available for purchase as whole clams, but are instead sold cleaned and sectioned.

Salmon sushi.
James O. Fraioli

Yellowtail sashimi.
James O. Fraioli

Octopus sashimi.
James O. Fraioli

Shrimp heads.
James O. Fraioli

Cucumber shrimp rolls.
James O. Fraioli

Dragon roll.
James O. Fraioli

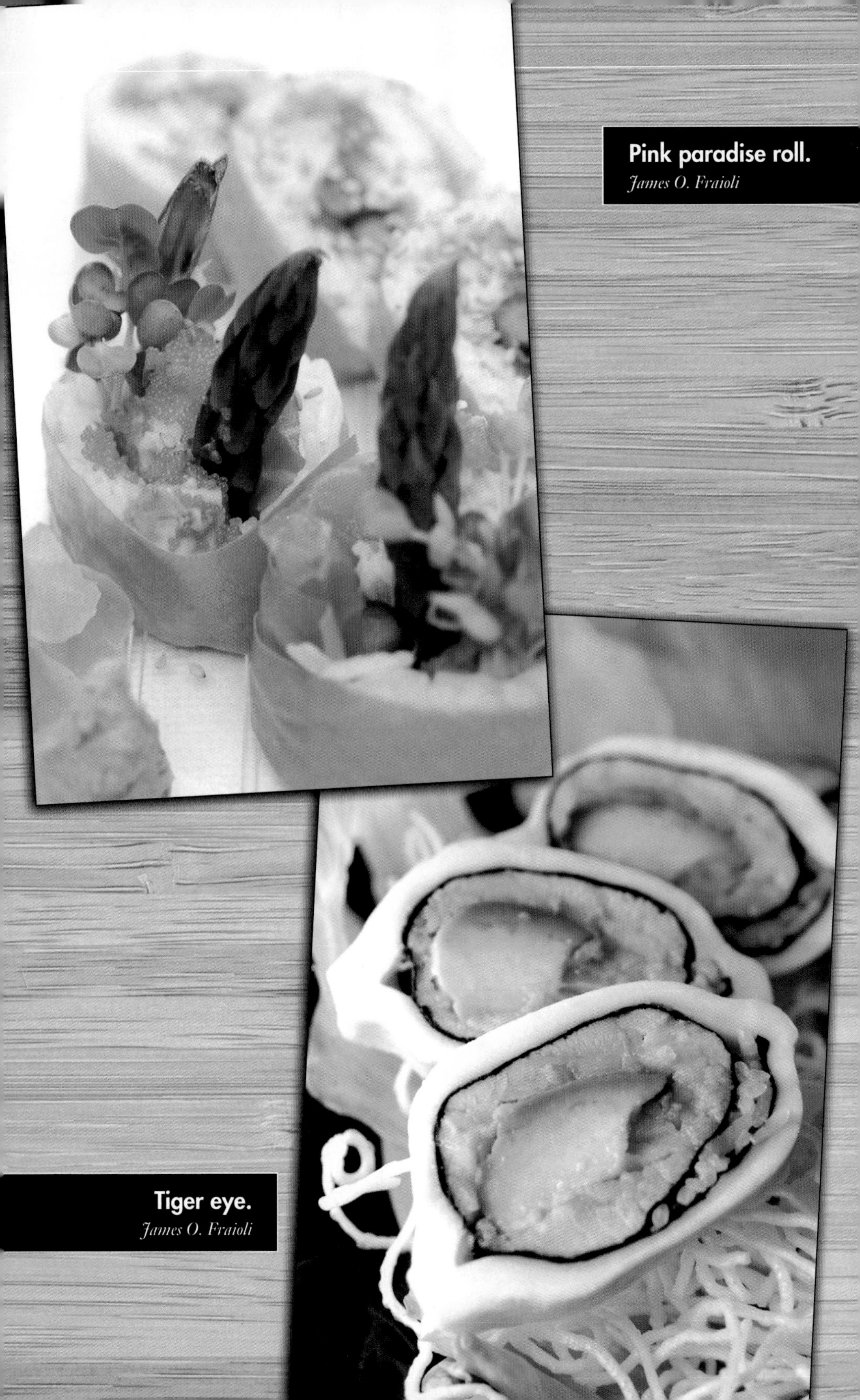

Pink paradise roll.
James O. Fraioli

Tiger eye.
James O. Fraioli

Spider roll.
James O. Fraioli

Tropical roll.
James O. Fraioli

Caterpillar roll.
James O. Fraioli

Moonshine roll.
James O. Fraioli

Big eyes sushi.
James O. Fraioli

Hawaiian poke.
James O. Fraioli

Volcano roll.
James O. Fraioli

Soft shell crab.
James O. Fraioli

Chapter 7

Sushi Rolls

In This Chapter

- Eighteen savory sushi rolls
- Pointers from the kitchen
- Appropriate garnishes

It's time to continue using that delicious rice you prepared in Chapter 4. Have it cooled and ready, along with the delicious seafood, fruits and vegetables you have chosen. Always prepare a variety of rolls so that your guests have plenty to choose from. Decide which rolls you will make, preferably using similar ingredients so that each roll compliments the next and the next compliments the last. When mixing ingredients, try to find a balance and make sure to take into consideration your guests' likes and dislikes. There are many sushi roll recipes to try; from the fiery Dragon Roll to the mild King Cobra Roll, so make sure to review them all.

To avoid having to clean your bamboo rolling mat after each use—and to eliminate any fish or rice sticking to the mat—always wrap the mat with plastic wrap prior to use.

Another helpful tip is to keep a sharp knife close by and always dip it into water before cutting a roll. A damp knife never sticks.

Eel Sauce

The sweet, hickory flavor of this sauce makes it perfect to drizzle over a number of sushi creations.

Makes 2 cups

½ cup sugar

½ cup water

½ cup soy sauce

½ cup Mirin sake

1. Combine sugar, water, soy sauce, and mirin sake in a small pot, and cook over high heat until boiling. Lower heat, and simmer until achieving a thick consistency of maple syrup, being careful not to burn the sauce while thickening. To help the process, add corn starch as a thickening agent.

Ponzu Sauce

Citrus-based Ponzu is a very tart dipping sauce used for sashimi.

Makes approximately 1 cup

1 TB. lemon juice

½ cup rice vinegar

½ cup water

½ cup soy sauce

¼ cup Mirin sake

Pinch of dry seaweed

Pinch of dried fish flakes

1. Mix lemon juice, vinegar, water, soy sauce and sake, and add seaweed and fish flakes.

Spicy Sauce

This is the perfect sauce for those looking for a little extra kick.

Makes 1 cup

1 cup Japanese mayonnaise (or regular mayonnaise)

Pinch chili powder

1 or 2 tsp. hot chili sauce, to taste

1 TB. sesame oil

½ cup soy sauce

1 scallion, finely chopped

Katsuobushi (dried fish shavings)

1. Combine and mix mayonnaise, chili powder, chili sauce, sesame oil, soy sauce, scallion, and katsuobushi. Add more soy sauce if mixture is too thick.

Crab Mixture

This mixture is used in many different sushi rolls to add color and flavor.

Makes 1 cup

1 cup shredded crab meat (snow, king, or Dungeness)

2 TB. Japanese mayonnaise (or regular mayonnaise)

1. Combine and mix crab meat and mayonnaise until moist. Add additional mayonnaise if need be.

Scallop and Crab Mixture

Adding scallops to the crab mixture creates a thicker texture.

Makes 1 cup

¼ cup shredded or diced scallops

¾ cup crab meat (snow, king, or Dungeness), shredded

2 TB. Japanese mayonnaise (or regular mayonnaise)

1. Combine and mix scallops, crab, and mayonnaise until moist. Add more mayonnaise if needed.

Spicy Scallop and Crab Mixture

For a more kicked up version of the previous recipe, do the following.

Makes 1 cup

¼ cup shredded or diced scallops

¾ cup crab meat (snow, king, or Dungeness), shredded

2 TB. Japanese mayonnaise (or regular mayonnaise)

1 or 2 TB. hot chili sauce, to taste

1. Combine and mix scallops, crab, and mayonnaise, and chili sauce until moist. Add more mayonnaise if needed.

Spicy Tuna Mixture

Like the spicy crab mixture, using this filling will add extra flavor that will leave your mouth and eyes watering.

Makes 1 cup

1 cup ahi-grade tuna, minced

1 or 2 tsp. hot chili sauce, to taste

1 scallion, finely diced

1. Combine and mix tuna, chili sauce, and scallion.

Alaskan Roll

Broad and flavorful, the Alaskan roll is a treat for the seafood lover.

Serving size: 5 to 6 slices

½ sheet *nori*, approximately 4×7-inches

¾ cup prepared sushi rice

Sesame seeds, as needed

2 pieces halibut, approximately 1-inch wide, 3-inches long and ¼-inch thick, sliced across grain with bones and skin removed

1 piece salmon, approximately 1-inch wide, 3-inches long and ¼-inch thick, sliced across grain with bones and skin removed

2 TB. scallop and crab mixture (recipe in this chapter)

1 TB. spicy sauce (recipe in this chapter)

1 thin slice avocado

Daikon radish sprouts *(kaiware)*, approximately 12 strands

½ cup smelt eggs or flying fish roe

1 TB. salmon eggs

1. Place nori in front of you, in a vertical position, shiny side down.
2. Spoon rice onto nori. Using your fingers, spread rice across sheet, covering edges. Press evenly and eliminate clumps. Leave 1-inch space with no rice on top of sheet.
3. Sprinkle rice with sesame seeds.
4. Flip sheet over so seaweed is facing up. Place halibut and salmon slices on lower half of rice (side closest to you).
5. Add ½ TB. spicy sauce above fish slices, building toward center; add 2 TB. scallop and crab mixture above sauce; add avocado slice above mixture; add daikon radish strands, with leaf petals hanging over edges outside roll.

6. Starting with side closest to you, tightly roll with your fingers.
7. Using a bamboo rolling mat (makisu), cover roll and gently squeeze firmly to compact roll.
8. Dip roll in a dish smelt eggs or flying fish roe, and roll so eggs stick to outer side of rice.
9. Using a sharp, damp knife, slice roll in 5 to 6 pieces, each approximately 1-inch thick.
10. Plate roll slices, and top each with a few salmon eggs.

California Roll

This is a refreshingly crisp roll due to the fresh avocado, crunchy cucumber, and firm crab meat.

Serving size: 8 slices

½ sheet *nori*, approximately 4×7-inches

¾ cup prepared sushi rice

Sesame seeds, as needed

2 thin slices avocado

1 long, slender strip cucumber, approximately 4-inches long with skin on

3 to 4 TB. crab mixture (recipe in this chapter)

½ cup smelt eggs or flying fish roe

1. Place nori in front of you, in a horizontal position, shiny side down.
2. Spoon rice onto nori. Using your fingers, spread rice across sheet, covering all edges. Press evenly to remove clumps.
3. Sprinkle rice with sesame seeds.
4. Flip sheet over so seaweed is facing up.
5. Place avocado slices on lower half of rice (side closer to you).
6. Add crab mixture above avocado; then add cucumber strip.
7. Starting with side closer to you, tightly roll with your fingers.
8. Using a bamboo rolling mat, cover roll, and gently squeeze firmly to compact roll.
9. Dip roll in a dish of smelt eggs, and roll so eggs stick to outer side of rice.
10. Using a sharp, damp knife, slice roll into 8 pieces, each approximately 1-inch thick.

From the Kitchen

In other parts of the world, such as in the Philippines, a slice of ripe mango is added to the roll for a bit of sweetness.

Caterpillar Roll

With avocado wrapped around the outer part of the roll, the different green and yellow hues make this roll look like the body of a caterpillar.

Serving size: 8 slices

½ sheet *nori*, approximately 4×7-inches

¾ cup prepared sushi rice

Sesame seeds, as needed

2 thin slices avocado, plus 4 additional slices cut in half (8 pieces)

1 long, slender strip cucumber, approximately 4-inches long with skin

3 to 4 TB. crab mixture (recipe in this chapter)

3 pieces roasted fresh water eel *(unagi)*

2 strands daikon radish sprouts *(kaiware)*

2 octopus tentacle suction cups

2 salmon eggs

2 black sesame seeds

Eel sauce, as needed (recipe in this chapter)

1. Place nori in front of you, in a horizontal position, shiny side down.
2. Spoon rice onto nori. Using your fingers, spread rice across sheet, covering all edges. Press evenly to remove clumps.
3. Sprinkle rice with sesame seeds.
4. Flip sheet over so seaweed is facing up.
5. Place avocado slices on lower half of rice (side closer to you).
6. Add crab mixture above avocado; then add cucumber strip.
7. Roast eel by placing three pieces of prepackaged unagi approximately 1-inch wide by 3-inches long on a baking sheet lined with foil. Do not remove skin. Roast in a toaster oven or under the broiler until hot and slightly charred. Remove and add to roll, above cucumber.

8. Starting with side closer to you, tightly roll with your fingers.
9. Place half-slices avocado on roll.
10. Tear a sheet of plastic wrap and cover roll, which will ensure that nothing sticks together. Using the bamboo rolling mat, cover roll, and gently squeeze firmly to compact roll.
11. Keeping the plastic wrap over roll, slice roll (through the plastic) with a sharp, damp knife into 8 pieces, each approximately 1-inch thick.
12. Remove the plastic wrap from roll, and align sections on a plate to resemble the body of a caterpillar. At one end, poke two holes in the last piece of sushi, and insert two strands of daikon radish for antenna (the head). Add two octopus suction cups from an octopus tentacle below the antenna. Inside each suction cup, add one salmon egg and one black sesame seed to create the eyes and pupils.
13. Top roll with drizzle of eel sauce.

Dragon Roll

Besides spicy tuna, eel is another popular seafood to use for this roll.

Serving size: 8 slices

½ sheet *nori*, approximately 4×7-inches

¾ cup prepared sushi rice

Sesame seeds, as needed

1 tempura asparagus spear, approximately 4-inches long

3 to 4 TB. crab mixture (recipe in this chapter)

4 thin slices tuna or any desired fish

Scallions, finely chopped, to taste

Hot chili sauce, to taste

Ponzu sauce, as needed (recipe in this chapter)

1. Place nori in front of you, in a horizontal position, shiny side down.
2. Spoon rice onto nori. Using your fingers, spread rice across sheet, covering all edges. Press evenly to remove clumps.
3. Sprinkle rice with sesame seeds.
4. Flip sheet over so seaweed is facing up.
5. Make tempura asparagus by dusting spear in flour and shaking off excess. Next, roll spear in tempura batter (prepare according to package directions), and deep fry in hot oil until golden brown. Remove spear from oil, pat dry with paper towel, and cool.
6. Place tempura asparagus spear on lower half of rice (side closer to you).
7. Add crab mixture above asparagus.
8. Starting with side closer to you, tightly roll with your fingers.
9. Add tuna slices to roll.

10. Tear a sheet of plastic wrap and cover the roll, which will ensure that nothing sticks together. Using the bamboo rolling mat, cover roll and gently squeeze firmly to compact roll.
11. Keeping the plastic wrap over the roll, slice roll (through the plastic) with a sharp, damp knife into 8 pieces, each approximately 1-inch thick.
12. Remove the plastic wrap, and plate roll, topping each slice with scallions, drizzle of chili sauce, and drizzle of Ponzu sauce.

From the Kitchen

For those who enjoy creativity, cut and reline the roll in a shape of a dragon. You can also use your imagination and make dragon eyes from tobiko and antennae from carrot sticks.

Indian Roll

This is similar to a California roll, but also features fresh shrimp.

Serving size: 5 to 6 slices

½ sheet *nori*, approximately 4×7-inches

¾ cup prepared sushi rice

Sesame seeds, as needed

2 cooked shrimp, butterflied

1 thin slice avocado

1 long, slender strip cucumber, approximately 4-inches long with skin

3 to 4 TB. crab mixture (recipe in this chapter)

Daikon radish sprouts *(kaiware)*, approximately 12 strands

1 TB. spicy sauce (recipe in this chapter)

1. Place nori in front of you, in a vertical position, shiny side down.
2. Spoon rice onto nori. Using your fingers, spread rice across sheet, covering all edges. Press evenly to remove clumps. Leave 1-inch space with no rice on top.
3. Sprinkle rice with sesame seeds.
4. Prepare shrimp by sliding a metal or bamboo skewer through length of large tail sections (with shell on). The skewer will prohibit tails from curling when cooked. Place the skewer in a pot of boiling water until tails are pink and tender. Immediately dip tails in an ice water bath to stop the cooking process. Remove tails from the skewer, discard shells, and butterfly each by slicing through tail with a sharp knife so tail lies flat. Do not cut all the way through.
5. Place shrimp tails on lower half of rice (side closer to you).
6. Add avocado, cucumber, and crab mixture. Add radish strands, with leaf petals hanging over edges outside roll. Finish by adding spicy sauce.

7. Starting with side closer to you, tightly roll with your fingers.
8. Using the bamboo rolling mat, cover roll and gently squeeze firmly to compact roll.
9. Using a sharp, damp knife, slice roll into 5 to 6 pieces, each approximately 1-inch thick, and plate.

King Cobra Roll

This roll has a delicate flavor that will be enhanced by your choice of the regular or spicy eel sauce.

Serving size: 8 slices

½ sheet *nori*, approximately 4×7-inches

¾ cup prepared sushi rice

Sesame seeds, as needed

2 thin slices avocado, plus 4 additional slices

1 tempura shrimp, halved lengthwise

2 or 3 TB. crab mixture (recipe in this chapter)

½ cup tempura crumbs

4 pieces roasted fresh water eel (*unagi*)

Eel sauce, to taste (recipe in this chapter)

1. Place nori in front of you, in a horizontal position, shiny side down.
2. Spoon rice onto nori. Using your fingers, spread rice across sheet, covering all edges. Press evenly to remove clumps.
3. Sprinkle rice with sesame seeds.
4. Flip sheet over so seaweed is facing up.
5. Place avocado slices on lower half of rice (side closer to you).
6. Prepare tempura shrimp by removing tail meat from one large shrimp or prawn. Discard shell and devein if necessary. Dust shrimp in flour, shaking off excess. Roll shrimp in tempura batter (prepare according to package directions), and deep fry in hot oil until golden brown. Remove shrimp from oil, and cut in half lengthwise.
7. Add shrimp pieces above avocado and cucumber; add crab mixture.
8. Starting with side closer to you, tightly roll with your fingers.
9. Using the bamboo rolling mat, cover roll, and gently squeeze firmly to compact roll.

10. Tear a sheet of plastic wrap and place on counter. Spread tempura crumbs on the sheet, and add roll. Coat thoroughly with crumbs.
11. Top roll with additional avocado slices, and set aside.
12. Roast eel by placing four pieces of prepackaged unagi approximately 1-inch wide by 3-inches long on a baking sheet lined with foil. Do not remove skin. Roast in a toaster oven or under the broiler until hot and slightly charred.
13. Add roasted eel and avocado, side by side.
14. Cover with plastic wrap, and slice roll with a sharp, damp knife into 8 pieces, each approximately 1-inch thick, drizzle with eel sauce and plate.

From the Kitchen

Like the Dragon Roll, show off your creativity by cutting and relining the roll in a shape of a snake. Make the eyes from tobiko and the forked tongue from a carrot stick.

Local Roll

Complimentary to the Montecito Roll, the Local Roll is commonly served in a less formal setting.

Serving size: 5 to 6 slices

½ sheet *nori*, approximately 4×7-inches

¾ cup prepared sushi rice

Sesame seeds, as needed

2 pieces tempura halibut

1 thin slice avocado

1 long, slender strip cucumber, approximately 4-inches long with skin on

3 to 4 TB. crab mixture (recipe in this chapter)

Daikon radish sprouts *(kaiware)*, approximately 12 strands

1 TB. spicy sauce (recipe in this chapter)

1. Place nori in front of you, in a vertical position, shiny side down.
2. Spoon rice onto nori. Using your fingers, spread rice across sheet, covering all edges. Press evenly to remove clumps. Leave a 1-inch space with no rice on top of sheet.
3. Sprinkle rice with sesame seeds.
4. Prepare tempura halibut by dusting two thin slices, 1-inch by 3-inches, in flour, shaking off excess. Next, roll halibut in tempura batter (prepare according to package directions), and deep fry in hot oil until golden brown. Remove halibut from oil.
5. Place halibut on lower half of rice (side closer to you).
6. Add avocado, cucumber, and crab mixture. Add radish strands, with petals hanging over edges outside roll. Finish by adding spicy sauce.
7. Starting with side closer to you, tightly roll with your fingers.

8. Using the bamboo rolling mat, cover roll and gently squeeze firmly to compact roll.
9. Slice roll with a sharp, damp knife into 5 to 6 pieces, each approximately 1-inch thick, and plate.

Montecito Roll

Fabulous for serving at a formal engagement, this roll is stylish and sophisticated.

Serving size: 5 to 6 slices

½ sheet *nori*, approximately 4×7-inches

¾ cup prepared sushi rice

Sesame seeds, as needed

1 or 2 pieces cooked lobster tail meat, approximately 1×4 inches, thinly sliced

1 thin slice avocado

1 long, slender strip cucumber, approximately 4-inches long with skin on

3 to 4 TB. crab mixture (recipe in this chapter)

Daikon radish sprouts *(kaiware)*, approximately 12 strands

1 TB. spicy sauce (recipe in this chapter)

1 tsp. smelt eggs or flying fish roe

1. Place nori in front of you, in a vertical position, shiny side down.
2. Spoon rice onto nori. Using your fingers, evenly spread rice across sheet, covering edges and removing clumps. Leave a 1-inch space with no rice on top of sheet.
3. Sprinkle rice with sesame seeds.
4. Place lobster on lower half of rice (side closer to you). To prepare lobster, boil tail or live lobster in salted boiling water until shell turns red and meat is opaque and tender.
5. Add avocado, cucumber, and crab mixture. Add radish strands, with petals hanging over edges outside roll. Finish by adding spicy sauce and smelt eggs.
6. Starting with side closer to you, tightly roll with your fingers.

7. Using the bamboo mat, gently squeeze firmly to compact roll.
8. Slice roll with a sharp, damp knife into 5 to 6 pieces, each approximately 1-inch thick, and plate.

Fish Facts

The Montecito Roll is named after the California spiny lobster, a popular resident off the shores of Montecito, California. For those unable to purchase fresh California lobster, Maine lobster is equally delicious.

Moonlight Roll

From preparation to serving, this roll goes great with a night of fun.

Serving size: 8 slices

½ sheet *nori*, approximately 4×7-inches

¾ cup prepared sushi rice

Sesame seeds, as needed

2 thin slices avocado

3 to 4 TB. crab mixture (recipe in this chapter)

1 long, slender strip cucumber, approximately 4-inches long with skin on

½ cup smelt eggs or flying fish roe

3 to 4 TB. spicy scallop and crab mixture (recipe in this chapter)

1. Place nori in front of you, in a horizontal position, shiny side down.
2. Spoon rice onto nori. Using your fingers, spread rice across sheet, covering edges and pressing evenly to remove clumps.
3. Sprinkle rice with sesame seeds.
4. Flip sheet over so seaweed is facing up.
5. Place avocado slices on lower half of rice (side closer to you).
6. Add crab mixture above avocado, and add cucumber strip.
7. Starting with the side closer to you, tightly roll with your fingers.
8. Using the bamboo rolling mat, cover roll and gently squeeze firmly to compact roll.
9. Dip roll in smelt eggs or fish roe, and roll so eggs stick to outer side of rice.
10. Slice roll with a sharp, damp knife into 8 pieces, each approximately 1-inch thick.

11. Arrange slices, face up, on a baking sheet lined with foil. Top each slice with dollop of spicy scallop and crab mixture.
12. Bake slices in a toaster over or under the broiler until golden brown.

Moonshine Roll

The sweetness of the papaya compliments the vegetables and the shrimp splendidly.

Serving size: 8 slices

½ sheet (green) Mame*nori*, Soybean Paper, approximately 4×7-inches

¾ cup prepared sushi rice

Sesame seeds, as needed

2 cooked shrimp, butterflied

2 thin slices avocado

1 thin slice papaya

2 steamed asparagus spears, approximately 4-inches long

Daikon radish sprouts *(kaiware)*, approximately 12 strands

1. Place soybean paper in front of you in a vertical position.
2. Spoon rice onto paper. Using your fingers, spread rice across the sheet, covering edges and pressing evenly to remove clumps. Leave a 1-inch space with no rice on top of sheet.
3. Sprinkle rice with sesame seeds.
4. Prepare shrimp by sliding a metal or bamboo skewer through length of tail sections with shell on. The skewer will prohibit tails from curling when cooked. Place the skewer in a pot of boiling water until tails are pink and tender. Immediately dip tails in an ice water bath to stop the cooking process. Remove tails from the skewer, discard shells, and butterfly by slicing through each tail until it lies flat. Do not cut all the way through.
5. Place shrimp on lower half of rice (side closer to you).
6. Add avocado, papaya, and asparagus spears.
7. Add radish strands, with petals hanging over edges outside roll.

8. Starting with the side closer to you, tightly roll with your fingers.
9. Using the bamboo rolling mat, cover roll and gently squeeze firmly to compact roll.
10. Slice roll with a sharp, damp knife into 8 pieces, each approximately 1-inch thick, and plate.

Food Corner

Mamenori Soybean Paper comes in a variety of colors including pink, yellow, orange, green and natural. Although the Moonshine Roll is made with green paper, try different colors for added excitement.

Pink Paradise Roll

Don't be intimidated by the numerous ingredients—it is surprisingly simple to make!

Serving size: 5 to 6 slices

½ sheet (pink) Mame*nori*, Soybean Paper, approximately 4×7-inches

¾ cup prepared sushi rice

Sesame seeds, as needed

2 cooked shrimp, butterflied

1 piece salmon, approximately 1-inch wide, 3-inches long, and ¼-inch thick, sliced across grain with bones and skin removed

2 thin slices avocado

2 or 3 TB. crab mixture (recipe in this chapter)

1 TB. smelt eggs or flying fish roe

1 long, slender strip cucumber, approximately 4-inches long with skin on

1 or 2 steamed asparagus spears, approximately 4-inches long

Daikon radish sprouts *(kaiware)*, approximately 12 strands

1. Place soybean paper in front of you in a vertical position.
2. Spoon rice onto paper. Using your fingers, spread rice across the sheet, covering edges and removing clumps. Leave a 1-inch space with no rice on top of sheet.
3. Sprinkle rice with sesame seeds.
4. Prepare shrimp by sliding a metal or bamboo skewer through length of tail sections with shell on. The skewer will prohibit tails from curling when cooked. Place the skewer in a pot of boiling water until tails are pink and tender. Immediately dip tails in an ice water bath to stop the cooking process. Remove tails from the skewer, discard shells, and butterfly each by slicing through tail until it lies flat. Do not cut all the way through.

5. Place shrimp tails on lower half of rice (side closer to you).
6. Add salmon, avocado, crab mixture, smelt eggs, cucumber, and asparagus.
7. Add radish strands with petals hanging over edges outside roll.
8. Starting with the side closer to you, tightly roll with your fingers.
9. Using the bamboo rolling mat, cover roll and gently squeeze firmly to compact roll.
10. Slice roll with a sharp, damp knife into 5 or 6 pieces, each approximately 1-inch thick, and plate.

Rainbow Roll

This roll is an eclectic collection of colors and flavors.

Serving size: 8 slices

½ sheet *nori*, approximately 4×7-inches

¾ cup prepared sushi rice

Sesame seeds, as needed

2 thin slices avocado

3 to 4 TB. crab mixture (recipe in this chapter)

1 long, slender strip cucumber, approximately 4-inches long with skin on

1 slice each 5 varying colored fish (example: tuna, salmon, shrimp, halibut, and yellowtail)

1. Place nori in front of you, in a horizontal position, shiny side down.
2. Spoon rice onto nori. Using your fingers, spread rice across sheet, covering edges and pressing evenly to remove clumps.
3. Sprinkle rice with sesame seeds.
4. Flip sheet over so seaweed is facing up.
5. Place avocado slices on lower half of rice (side closer to you).
6. Add crab mixture above avocado, and add cucumber.
7. Starting with side closer to you, tightly roll with your fingers.
8. Using the bamboo rolling mat, cover roll and gently squeeze firmly to compact roll.
9. Alternate fish slices with avocado slices on roll, creating a seafood rainbow.
10. Cover roll with a sheet of plastic wrap, which will ensure that nothing sticks together. Using the bamboo rolling mat, gently squeeze firmly to compact roll.

11. Keeping the plastic wrap over roll, slice roll (through the plastic) with a sharp, damp knife into 8 pieces, each approximately 1-inch thick, and plate.

Food Corner

The Rainbow Roll is named after the alternating colors of the seafood used. Try and choose bright and contrasting colors when selecting your fish.

Samurai Roll

The perfection of this roll will bring much honor to the sushi chef.

½ sheet (green) Mamenori, Soybean Paper, approximately 4×7-inches

¾ cup prepared sushi rice

Sesame seeds, as needed

2 tempura asparagus spears, approximately 4-inches long

1 thin slice avocado

2 or 3 TB. crab mixture (recipe in this chapter)

2 or 3 TB. spicy tuna mixture (recipe in this chapter)

Daikon radish sprouts *(kaiware)*, approximately 12 strands

Serving size: 5 to 6 slices

1. Place soybean paper in front of you, in a vertical position.
2. Spoon rice onto paper. Using your fingers, spread rice across sheet, covering edges and removing clumps. Leave a 1-inch space with no rice on top of sheet.
3. Sprinkle rice with sesame seeds.
4. Prepare tempura asparagus by dusting spears in flour and shaking off excess. Next, roll spears in tempura batter (prepare according to package directions), and deep fry in hot oil until golden brown. Remove spears from oil.
5. Place asparagus spears on lower half of rice (side closer to you).
6. Add avocado slice, crab meat mixture, and spicy tuna mixture.
7. Add radish strands, with petals hanging over edges outside roll.
8. Starting with the side closer to you, tightly roll with your fingers.

9. Using the bamboo rolling mat, cover roll and gently squeeze firmly to compact roll.

10. Slice roll with a sharp, damp knife into 5 or 6 pieces, each approximately 1-inch thick, and plate.

Snake Roll

Similar to the Rainbow Roll, the Snake roll uses eel instead of several varying types of fish.

Serving size: 8 slices

½ sheet *nori*, approximately 4×7-inches

¾ cup prepared sushi rice

Sesame seeds, as needed

2 thin slices avocado

3 to 4 TB. crab mixture (recipe in this chapter)

1 long, slender strip cucumber, approximately 4-inches long with skin on

3 pieces roasted fresh water eel *(unagi)*

Eel sauce, to taste (recipe in this chapter)

1. Place nori in front of you, in a horizontal position, shiny side down.
2. Spoon rice onto nori. Using your fingers, spread rice across sheet, covering edges and removing clumps.
3. Sprinkle rice with sesame seeds.
4. Flip sheet over so seaweed is facing up.
5. Place avocado slices on lower half of rice (side closer to you).
6. Add crab mixture above avocado, and add cucumber strip.
7. Starting with side closer to you, tightly roll with your fingers.
8. Using the bamboo rolling mat, cover roll and gently squeeze firmly to compact roll.
9. Roast eel by placing three pieces prepackaged unagi approximately 1-inch wide by 3-inches long on a baking sheet lined with foil. Don't remove skin. Roast in a toaster oven or under the broiler until hot and slightly charred. Remove eel, and place on roll.

10. Cover roll with a sheet of plastic wrap to ensure that nothing sticks together. Using the bamboo rolling mat, gently squeeze firmly to compact roll.
11. Slice roll (through the plastic) with a sharp, damp knife into 8 pieces, each approximately 1-inch thick.
12. Remove the plastic wrap, and plate roll. Top each slice with drizzle of eel sauce and sprinkle of sesame seeds.

Fish Facts

As for unagi itself, the best comes from fresh water eels that are wild caught and not bred in eel farms. Some fancy restaurants in Japan keep tanks full of live eels, which aren't prepared until the unagi is ordered.

Spicy Shrimp with Tuna & Jalapeño Roll

If you are looking to spice up your life, this is the roll for you.

Serving size: 8 slices

½ sheet *nori*, approximately 4×7-inches

¾ cup prepared sushi rice

Sesame seeds, as needed

3 cooked shrimp, butterflied

1 TB. spicy sauce (recipe in this chapter)

2 thin slices avocado

4 or 5 thin slices tuna

1 jalapeño, thinly sliced

1. Place nori in front of you, in a horizontal position, shiny side down.
2. Spoon rice onto nori. Using your fingers, spread rice across sheet, covering edges and removing clumps.
3. Sprinkle rice with sesame seeds.
4. Flip sheet over so seaweed is facing up.
5. To prepare shrimp, slide a metal or bamboo skewer through length of tail sections with shell on. The skewer will prohibit tails from curling when cooked. Place the skewer in a pot of boiling water until tails are pink and tender. Immediately dip tails in an ice water bath to stop the cooking process. Remove tails from the skewer, discard shells, and butterfly by slicing through each tail until it lies flat. Do not cut all the way through.
6. Place shrimp tails on lower half of rice (side closer to you). Add spicy sauce and avocado.
7. Starting with the side closer to you, tightly roll with your fingers; then using the bamboo rolling mat, cover roll and gently squeeze firmly to compact roll. Top roll with tuna slices.
8. Cover roll with a sheet of plastic wrap, which will ensure that nothing sticks together. Using the bamboo rolling mat, gently squeeze firmly to compact roll.

9. Keeping the plastic wrap intact, slice roll through the plastic with a sharp, damp knife into 8 pieces, each approximately 1-inch thick.
10. Remove the plastic wrap, and plate roll. Top each slice with jalapeño, and sprinkle with sesame seeds.

Spicy Tuna Roll

Fast and easy to prepare, this roll is short on prep-time, big on taste.

Serving size: 5 to 6 slices

½ sheet *nori*, approximately 4×7-inches

¾ cup prepared sushi rice

Sesame seeds, as needed

3 to 4 TB. spicy tuna mixture (recipe in this chapter)

Daikon radish sprouts *(kaiware)*, approximately 12 strands

1 TB. spicy sauce (recipe in this chapter)

1. Place nori in front of you, in a vertical position, shiny side down.
2. Spoon rice onto nori. Using your fingers, spread rice across sheet, covering edges and removing clumps. Leave a 1-inch space with no rice on top of sheet.
3. Sprinkle rice with sesame seeds.
4. Add tuna mixture to lower half of rice (side closer to you).
5. Add radish sprouts with petals hanging over edges outside roll. Finish by adding spicy sauce.
6. Starting with side closer to you, tightly roll with your fingers.
7. Using the bamboo rolling mat, cover roll and gently squeeze firmly to compact roll.
8. Using a sharp, damp knife, slice roll into 5 to 6 pieces, each approximately 1-inch thick, and plate.

From the Kitchen

The Spicy Tuna Roll varies from restaurant to restaurant because of the mixture of spices used. Some sushi bars prefer a dash of Japanese pepper while others insist on using spicy fish roe. Regardless of the spices used, this is one delicious roll!

Sun Rise Roll

The texture of the salmon and cream cheese is similar to the crab mixture, while adding the vegetables creates a flavor all its own.

Serving size: 5 to 6 slices

½ sheet (pink) Mame*nori*, Soybean Paper, approximately 4×7-inches

¾ cup prepared sushi rice

Sesame seeds, as needed

1 tempura asparagus spear, approximately 4-inches long

1 thin slice avocado

2 pieces smoked salmon, approx 1-inch wide and 4-inches long

1 oz. cream cheese, softened

Daikon radish sprouts *(kaiware)*, approximately 12 strands

1. Place soybean paper in front of you in a vertical position.
2. Spoon rice onto paper. Using your fingers, spread rice across sheet, covering edges and removing clumps. Leave a 1-inch space with no rice on top of sheet.
3. Sprinkle rice with sesame seeds.
4. Prepare asparagus by dusting with flour and shaking off excess. Roll spear in tempura batter (prepare according to package directions), and deep fry in hot oil until golden brown. Remove spear from oil, pat dry with paper towel, and cool.
5. Place spear on lower half of rice (side closer to you).
6. Add avocado, smoked salmon, and cream cheese.
7. Add radish sprouts with petals hanging over edges outside roll.
8. Starting with side closer to you, tightly roll with your fingers.
9. Using a sharp, damp knife, slice roll into 8 pieces, each approximately 1-inch thick, and plate.

Tokyo Roll

This nutritious roll is perfect for a unique summer snack.

Serving size: 5 to 6 slices

½ sheet (pink) Mamenori, Soybean Paper, approximately 4×7-inches

¾ cup prepared sushi rice

Sesame seeds, as needed

1 piece tempura banana, approximately 1-inch wide and 4-inches long

1 or 2 thin slices avocado

2 pieces roasted fresh water eel *(unagi)*

Eel sauce, to taste (recipe in this chapter)

1. Place soybean paper in front of you in a vertical position.
2. Spoon rice onto paper. Using your fingers, spread rice across sheet, covering edges and removing clumps. Leave a 1-inch space with no rice on top of sheet.
3. Sprinkle rice with sesame seeds.
4. Make tempura banana by dusting banana with flour and shaking off excess. Roll banana in tempura batter (prepare according to package directions), and deep fry in hot oil until golden brown. Remove banana from oil.
5. Place banana on lower half of rice (side closer to you). Add avocado slices.
6. Roast eel by placing prepackaged unagi approximately 1-inch wide by 3-inches long on a baking sheet lined with foil. Do not remove skin. Roast in a toaster oven or under the broiler until hot and slightly charred. Remove eel, and place beside avocado.
7. Starting with side closer to you, tightly roll with your fingers.

8. Using a sharp, damp knife, slice roll into 8 pieces, each approximately 1-inch thick.
9. Top each slice with drizzle of eel sauce and sprinkle of sesame seeds.

Food Corner

Always use ripe banana and not one that is overly ripe otherwise the tempura cooking process will make the banana very mushy. When it doubt, choose a banana that is just under-ripe so it will hold up in the hot oil.

Chapter 8

Cooked Rolls and Tempura Rolls

In This Chapter

- Eight delicious rolls
- Mastering the deep fryer
- Help from the kitchen

By now, you are more than likely becoming an expert at sushi and sashimi, but it's time to try something a little different. This chapter features recipes for cooked rolls and tempura rolls. You will learn tips on the proper cooking method that will create an end result that appeals to all the senses. These recipes are simple and do not require any difficult equipment. Besides a toaster oven and pots and pans, the preparation process is much like that of the previous recipes. These recipes may take a little longer to prepare, but they are definitely worth the extra time.

Unless you are making sushi for many guests, a toaster oven on your kitchen counter is very convenient and works best for baking the cooked rolls. For the tempura rolls, you don't need a cumbersome deep-fryer. A pot or deep-sided pan works just fine, especially since you will fry only one or two items at a time.

Tempura Shrimp

These cruchy shrimp are great on their own or as a tasty addition to sushi rolls.

Shrimp

Flour, as needed

Tempura batter (prepared according to package directions)

oil, as needed

1. Remove tail meat from shrimp. Discard shell and and devein if necessary.
2. Dust shrimp in flour and shake off excess.
3. Roll shrimp in tempura batter, and deep fry in hot oil until golden brown.
4. If shrimp are being used in a sushi roll, cut in half lengthwise.

Crunchy Roll

A great recipe to start with for someone who still has only a few rolls under their belt.

Serving size: 8 slices

½ sheet *nori*, approximately 4×7-inches

¾ cup prepared sushi rice

Sesame seeds, as needed

2 thin slices avocado

1 tempura shrimp, halved lengthwise (recipe in this chapter)

½ cup tempura crumbs

Eel sauce, as needed (recipe in Chapter 7)

1. Place nori in front of you, in a horizontal position, shiny side down, and spoon rice onto seaweed. Using your fingers, spread rice across sheet, covering edges and removing clumps. Sprinkle rice with sesame seeds.
2. Flip sheet over so nori is facing up, and place avocado slices on lower half of rice (side closer to you).
3. Add shrimp above avocado. Then, starting with side closer to you, tightly roll with your fingers.
4. Using the bamboo rolling mat, cover roll and gently squeeze firmly to compact.
5. Place a sheet of plastic wrap on the counter. Spread tempura crumbs on sheet and add roll. Coat roll thoroughly with crumbs. Roll the plastic wrap, and with a sharp, damp knife, slice roll into 8 pieces, each approximately 1-inch thick.
6. Remove the plastic wrap, plate roll, and top with drizzle of Eel sauce.

From the Kitchen

Traditionally, unagi is eaten in Japan during the hottest days of summer, usually in late July. This is because Japanese believe unagi provides them with strength and vitality for the rest of the year.

Eel Roll

This one warms your insides up on the cooler days and keeps you going on the hot ones.

Serving size: 5 to 6 slices

½ sheet *nori*, approximately 4×7-inches

¾ cup prepared sushi rice

Sesame seeds, as needed

3 pieces fresh water eel *(unagi)*

1 thin slice avocado

1 long, slender strip cucumber, approximately 4-inches long with skin

Eel sauce, as needed (recipe in Chapter 7)

1. After placing the sheet of nori in front of you, in a vertical position, shiny side down, spoon rice onto seaweed. Using your fingers, spread rice across the sheet, covering all edges and working out clumps. Leave a 1-inch space with no rice on top of the sheet.
2. Sprinkle rice with sesame seeds.
3. Roast eel by placing prepackaged unagi approximately 1-inch wide by 3-inches long on a baking sheet lined with foil. Do not remove skin. Roast in a toaster oven or under the broiler until hot and slightly charred. Remove eel and place on the lower half of rice, the side closer to you.
4. Place avocado and cucumber slices above eel. Then, starting with the side closer to you, tightly roll with your fingers.
5. Using the bamboo rolling mat, cover roll and gently squeeze firmly to compact.
6. Using a sharp, damp knife, slice roll in 5 to 6 pieces, each approximately 1-inch thick, top each slice with Eel sauce, and plate.

Philadelphia Roll

With its mild flavor, this roll is ideal for beginners who are wary of the more overpowering essence.

Serving size: 8 pieces

½ sheet *nori*, approximately 4×7-inches

¾ cup prepared sushi rice

1 oz. soft cream cheese

2 pieces salmon, approximately 1-inch thick and 4-inches long

Sesame seeds, as needed

2 thin slices avocado

1 long, slender strip cucumber, approximately 4-inches long with skin

Daikon radish sprouts *(kaiware)*, approximately 12 strands

1. Place nori in front of you, in a horizontal position, shiny side down.
2. Spoon rice onto nori. Using your fingers, spread rice across sheet, covering edges and smoothing clumps. Sprinkle rice with sesame seeds.
3. Flip sheet so seaweed is facing up, and spread cream cheese on the lower half.
4. Alongside cream cheese, add cooked salmon. To cook salmon, place pieces on a baking sheet lined with foil and place in a toaster oven or under the broiler until flesh is opaque. Do not overcook.
5. Add avocado and cucumber slice beside salmon. Add radish sprouts with petals hanging over edges outside roll.
6. Starting with side closer to you, tightly roll with your fingers. The rice will be on the outside. Cover roll with the bamboo rolling mat and gently squeeze firmly to compact roll.
7. Using a sharp, damp knife, slice roll into 6 to 8 slices and plate.

Salmon Skin Roll

The vegetables of the Salmon Skin Rolls are salty and sweet, while the salmon provides a smoky flavor.

Serving size: 8 slices

½ sheet *nori*, approximately 4×7-inches

¾ cup prepared sushi rice

Sesame seeds, as needed

3 TB. salmon skin

1 thin slice avocado

1 long, slender strip cucumber, approximately 4-inches long with skin

Daikon radish sprouts *(kaiware)*, approximately 12 strands

1 pickled gobo root (a.k.a. mountain burdock or *yamagobo*)

Katsuobushi (dried fish shavings), as needed

1. Place nori in front of you, in a vertical position, shiny side down, and spoon rice on top. Using your fingers, spread rice covering edges and removing clumps. Leave a 1-inch space with no rice on top of sheet.
2. Sprinkle rice with sesame seeds. Then flip sheet so nori is facing up.
3. Prepare salmon skin by removing a section approximately 4-inches wide and 6-inches long from salmon filet. Sprinkle skin with salt, and place on a baking sheet lined with foil. Roast in a toaster oven or under the broiler until skin is crispy. Remove from heat, and finely chop skin with a knife.
4. Add roasted salmon skin, avocado and cucumber slices, and gobo root (whole). Then add radish sprouts with petals hanging over edges outside roll.
5. Starting with side closer to you, tightly roll with your fingers. Rice will be on the outside. Cover roll with the bamboo rolling mat, and gently squeeze firmly to compact roll.

6. Place a sheet of plastic wrap on the counter, spread dried fish shavings on the sheet, and add roll, coating roll thoroughly with shavings. Roll the plastic wrap, and with a sharp, damp knife, slice roll in 8 pieces, each approximately 1-inch thick, and plate.

Fish Facts

Salmon skin does not reflect the intrinsic qualities of the particular fish it came from because the salmon's flesh and skin color vary from region to region, and between species.

Shrimp Tempura Roll

A very popular dish, the Shrimp Tempura Roll can be enjoyed by everyone.

Serving size: 5 to 6 slices

½ sheet *nori*, approximately 4×7-inches

¾ cup prepared sushi rice

Sesame seeds, as needed

2 pieces tempura shrimp (recipe in this chapter)

1 thin slice avocado

1 long, slender strip cucumber, approximately 4-inches long with skin

3 to 4 TB. crab mixture (recipe in Chapter 7)

Daikon radish sprouts *(kaiware)*, approximately 12 strands

1 TB. spicy sauce (recipe in Chapter 7)

1. Place nori in front of you, in a vertical position, shiny side down, and spoon rice on top of the nori. Using your fingers, spread rice covering all edges and removing clumps. Leave a 1-inch space with no rice on top of sheet.
2. Sprinkle rice with sesame seeds.
3. Place shrimp on lower half of rice, side closer to you. Add avocado and cucumber and crab mixture. Add radish sprouts with petals hanging over edges outside roll. Finish by adding Spicy Sauce.

4. Starting with side closer to you, tightly roll with your fingers. Then using the bamboo rolling mat, cover roll and gently squeeze firmly to compact.
5. Using a sharp, damp knife, slice roll into 5 to 6 pieces, each approximately 1-inch thick, and plate.

Spider Roll

Crunchy and creamy texture for a well-balanced sashimi.

Serving size: 5 to 6 slices

½ sheet *nori*, approximately 4×7-inches

¾ cup prepared sushi rice

Sesame seeds, as needed

1 soft shell crab, cut in half (recipe in Chapter 10)

1 thin slice avocado

1 long, slender strip cucumber, approximately 4-inches long with skin

3 to 4 TB. crab mixture (recipe in Chapter 7)

Daikon radish sprouts *(kaiware)*, approximately 12 strands

1 TB. Spicy Sauce, plus 2 TB. for garnish (recipe in Chapter 7)

Black sesame seeds, for garnish

1. Place nori in front of you, in a vertical position, shiny side down.
2. Spoon rice on seaweed. Using your fingers, spread rice across sheet, covering edges and removing clumps. Leave a 1-inch space with no rice at top of sheet. Sprinkle rice with sesame seeds.
3. Place crab on lower half of rice (side closer to you).
4. Add avocado, cucumber, and crab mixture. Add radish sprouts, with petals hanging over edges of roll. Finish by adding Spicy Sauce.
5. Starting with side closer to you, tightly roll with your fingers. Then cover roll with the bamboo rolling mat and gently squeeze firmly to compact.

6. Using a sharp, damp knife, slice roll into 5 to 6 pieces, each approximately 1-inch thick. Plate slices, and garnish with pool of spicy sauce sprinkled with black sesame seeds.

Food Corner

Fresh soft shelled crabs should be eaten within three or four days of molting, otherwise their shell begins to harden. During this stage, the crabs are called "papershells" and are much more crunchy to the palate.

Stuffed Calamari Roll

The Stuffed Calamari Roll is a worthwhile challenge, especially for the more adventurous chef.

Serving size: 6 slices

½ sheet *nori*, approximately 4×7-inches

1 TB. prepared sushi rice

3 or 4 TB. crab mixture (recipe in Chapter 7)

1 TB. flying fish roe or smelt eggs

2 strips scrambled egg, approximately ½-inch wide and 4-inches long

1 thin slice avocado

1 asparagus spear, steamed, approximately 4-inches long

1 fresh calamari steak, approximately 3-inches wide and 4-inches long

3 or 4 cups rice noodles, deep-fried

1 or 2 large green lettuce leaves

Eel sauce, as needed (recipe in Chapter 7)

1. Place nori in front of you, in a vertical position, shiny side down. Spoon rice onto nori. Using your fingers, spread rice, leaving a 1-inch space with no rice at top.
2. Place crab mixture on lower half of sheet. Add fish roe on top of crab.
3. In middle of sheet, add scrambled egg. To make egg, simply crack 1 egg and whisk in a bowl. Add pinch of salt and pinch of sugar. Pour into a nonstick fry pan over medium heat and scramble. Remove from heat; when cool, form egg with your fingers to create long strips.
4. Add avocado and asparagus beside egg; then starting at bottom, tightly roll with your fingers. Set aside.

5. With a sharp damp knife, insert the blade into side of calamari steak and open center creating a large pouch. Do not cut ends, keeping pouch intact. Place roll inside pouch.

6. Place calamari roll onto a baking sheet lined with foil. Bake in a toaster oven or under the broiler for 3 to 4 minutes. Turn roll, and cook for another 2 to 3 minutes. Do not overcook as calamari will be chewy and tough.

7. Remove roll, slice into 5 or 6 pieces using the sharp, damp knife, and set aside.

8. On a large plate, mound rice noodles. On top of noodles, place lettuce leaves. Arrange roll slices on leaves, and finish with drizzle of eel sauce.

Torpedo Roll

This intricately constructed roll is a great way to blend cooked and raw sashimi in a beautiful package.

Serving size: 8 to 10 slices

½ sheet *nori*, approximately 4×7-inches

½ sheet (pink) Mamenori soybean paper, approximately 4×7-inches

¾ cup prepared sushi rice

Sesame seeds, as needed

2 thin slices avocado

3 to 4 TB. crab mixture (recipe in Chapter 7)

1 long, slender strip cucumber, approximately 4-inches long with skin

4 or 5 thin slices halibut, approximately 1-inch wide by 4-inches long

Flour for dusting

2 eggs, beaten for egg wash

Panko crumbs, as needed

Spicy Sauce, as needed (recipe in Chapter 7)

1. Place nori in front of you, in a horizontal position, shiny side down, and spoon rice on top. Using your fingers, spread rice, covering edges and removing clumps. Sprinkle rice with sesame seeds.
2. Flip sheet over so nori is facing up, and place avocado slices on lower half of sheet, side closer to you.
3. Add crab mixture above avocado, and add cucumber strip.
4. Starting with side closer to you, tightly roll with your fingers. Then use the bamboo rolling mat and cover roll gently squeezing firmly to compact roll.
5. Cover halibut and entire roll with pink soybean paper (now outer layer).

6. Gently roll in flour, shaking off excess. Next, dip roll in egg wash, then Panko crumbs, and deep fry in hot oil until golden brown. Remove roll, and slice roll into 8 to 10 pieces using a sharp, damp knife.
7. Arrange slices on a plate, and top with spicy sauce.

From the Kitchen

The Torpedo Roll is a very large roll, and is an excellent dish that will feed several people. Take your time in making it, as the roll calls for many ingredients.

Chapter 9

Vegetarian Recipes

In This Chapter

- Nine veggie delights
- Fruit and vegetable tips
- Plating the perfect roll

Marvelous vegetarian recipes that will tickle the taste buds. When preparing these rolls for yourself or for your guests, you will have the opportunity to select your favorite fruits and vegetables in a new and exciting way. Along with your wonderfully prepared sushi rice, feel free to add a variety of garden vegetables that you might already have in the kitchen. If you're in the mood for something a little different, and ready for a trip to a Japanese food market, try a roll that calls for specialty items such as gobo root, an exciting ingredient packed with flavor.

Avocado Roll

A basic vegetable roll, the avocado roll is a great alternative to many of the seafood rolls.

Serving size: 6 slices

½ sheet *nori*, approximately 4×7-inches

¾ cup prepared sushi rice

Sesame seeds, as needed

2 slices fresh avocado

1. Place nori in front of you, in a horizontal position, shiny side down.
2. Spoon rice on nori. Using your fingers, spread rice, covering edges and eliminating clumps.
3. Sprinkle rice with sesame seeds, and place avocado slices on lower portion of rice.
4. Starting with side closer to you, tightly roll with your fingers. Using the bamboo rolling mat, cover roll and gently squeeze firmly to compact roll.
5. Slice roll with a sharp damp knife into 6 pieces, and plate.

Cucumber Roll

The Cucumber Roll is crisp and refreshing snack.

Serving size: 6 slices

½ sheet *nori*, approximately 4×7-inches

¾ cup prepared sushi rice

Sesame seeds, as needed

2 long, slender strips fresh cucumber, approximately 4-inches long with skin

1. Place nori in front of you, in a horizontal position, shiny side down.
2. Spoon rice on top of nori. Using your fingers, spread rice, covering all edges and pressing evenly to avoid clumps. Sprinkle rice with sesame seeds.
3. Place cucumber slices on lower portion of rice.
4. Starting with side closer to you, tightly roll with your fingers. Use the bamboo rolling mat and cover roll, gently squeezing firmly to compact the roll.
5. Slice roll with a sharp damp knife into 6 pieces, and plate.

Food Corner

The two popular cucumbers used in Japanese cuisine are the English cucumber and the Japanese cucumber. Of course, you can use a regular, locally-grown cucumber should you have one on hand.

Futomaki Roll

A more complex version of the Egg Sushi or Omelet recipe, the Futomaki Roll includes a selection of Japanese specialty vegetables.

Serving size: 5 or 6 slices

½ sheet *nori*, approximately 4×7-inches

¾ cup prepared sushi rice

Sesame seeds, as needed

1 TB. very fine fish flakes, pink color

1 gobo root (a.k.a. mountain burdock; *yamagobo*), whole

1 piece kanpyo

1 large piece shiitake mushroom, cooked

2 slender strips cucumber, approximately 4-inches long with skin

2 pieces scrambled egg, approximately ½-inch wide and 4-inches long

1. Place nori in front of you, in a vertical position, shiny side down.
2. Spoon rice onto top of nori. Using your fingers, spread rice, covering all edges and smoothing clumps. Leave a 1-inch space with no rice on top.
3. Sprinkle rice with sesame seeds. Add fish flakes to lower portion of rice.
4. Along side, add gobo root, kanpyo, mushroom, cucumber, and scrambled egg. To make egg, crack 1 egg and whisk in a bowl. Add pinch of salt and pinch of sugar. Pour into a nonstick fry pan over medium heat and scramble. Remove from heat and cool. Form eggs with your fingers to create long strips.
5. Starting with side closer to you, tightly roll with your fingers. Then use the bamboo rolling mat and cover roll; gently squeeze firmly to compact roll.
6. Using a sharp damp knife, slice roll into 5 or 6 pieces and plate.

Gobo Roll

The combined sweetness of the rice and pickled gobo is subtle yet satisfying.

Serving size: 6 slices

½ sheet *nori*, approximately 4×7-inches

¾ cup prepared sushi rice

Sesame seeds, as needed

2 pieces pickled gobo root (a.k.a. mountain burdock or *yamagobo*), whole

1. Place nori in front of you, in a horizontal position, shiny side down.
2. Spoon rice onto nori. Using your fingers, spread rice, covering edges and smoothing clumps. Sprinkle rice with sesame seeds. Place gobo root on lower portion of rice.
3. Starting with side closer to you, tightly roll with your fingers. Using the bamboo mat, gently squeeze firmly to compact roll.
4. Using a sharp damp knife, slice roll into 6 pieces and plate.

Food Corner

Gobo Root or Burdock Root is very crispy and has a sweet, mild pungent flavor. For the Gobo Roll, select pickled gobo root for more flavor.

Inari

This is the simplest form of this recipe, so feel free to experiment with additional ingredients.

Serving size: 2 pieces

2 pieces packaged deep-fried tofu (abura-age), each piece approximately 2-inches wide and 3-inches long

2 TB. prepared sushi rice

1. Open each piece tofu and create large pouch.
2. Inside each pouch, stuff 1 TB. rice.
3. Plate two pieces tofu together like sushi.

From the Kitchen

This dish is very sweet and can be served at the end of the meal like a dessert.

Ocean Salad Roll

If you are looking for a dish that is rich in nutrients the Ocean Salad Roll is a great place to find it.

Serving size: 5 or 6 slices

½ sheet *nori*, approximately 4×7-inches

¾ cup prepared sushi rice

Sesame seeds, as needed

3 or 4 TB. marinated seaweed *(wakame)*

1. Place nori in front of you, in a horizontal position.
2. Spoon rice onto nori. Using your fingers, spread rice, covering edges and smoothing clumps.
3. Sprinkle rice with sesame seeds. Spoon marinated seaweed on lower portion of rice.
4. Starting with side closer to you, tightly roll with your fingers. Use the bamboo mat, and gently squeeze firmly to compact roll.
5. Slice roll with a sharp damp knife into 5 to 6 pieces and plate.

Tropical Roll

This sushi roll is an exotic fruit cocktail wrapped in rice.

Serving size: 5 or 6 slices

½ sheet (pink) Mamenori soybean paper, approximately 4×7-inches

¾ cup prepared sushi rice

Sesame seeds, as needed

1 thin slice mango

1 thin slice papaya

1 thin slice avocado

1 banana slice, approximately 1-inch thick and 4-inches long

Flour for dusting

Tempura batter, as needed

Oil for deep frying

1. Place soybean paper in front of you, in a vertical position.
2. Spoon rice on top of it. Using your fingers, spread rice, covering edges and smoothing clumps. Leave 1-inch space with no rice at top.
3. Sprinkle rice with sesame seeds. Place mango, papaya, and avocado slice on lower half of rice (side closer to you).
4. To make tempura banana, dust banana with flour and shake off excess. Next, roll banana in tempura batter (prepare according to package), and deep fry in hot oil until golden brown. Remove banana.
5. Add tempura banana slice alongside avocado.
6. Starting with side closer to you, tightly roll with your fingers. Use the bamboo rolling mat and cover roll, gently squeezing firmly to compact roll.
7. Using a sharp damp knife, slice roll into 5 or 6 pieces and plate. Sprinkle with sesame seeds.

From the Kitchen

Feel free to experiment with other tropical fruits and see what you like best. Fruit alternatives that work well in this roll include: apricot, guava, kiwi, peach, star fruit, and various melon.

Vegetable Crunchy Roll

Tempura at its best, these highlighted veggies belong together in this crisp roll.

Serving size: 8 slices

½ sheet *nori*, approximately 4×7-inches

¾ cup prepared sushi rice

Sesame seeds, as needed

1 piece tempura asparagus, approximately 4-inches long

1 piece tempura broccoli, approximately 3-inches long

1 piece tempura zucchini, approximately 4-inches long

3 cups tempura crumbs

Eel sauce, as needed (recipe in Chapter 7)

1. Place nori in front of you, in a horizontal position, shiny side down.
2. Spoon rice on nori. Using your fingers, spread rice, covering edges and smoothing clumps. Sprinkle rice with sesame seeds. Flip sheet so seaweed is facing up.
3. Place asparagus, broccoli, and zucchini on lower portion. To make tempura vegetables, dust each piece with flour and shake off excess. Next dip into tempura batter (prepare according to package), and deep fry in hot oil until golden brown. Remove veggies, pat dry with paper towel, and cool.
4. Starting with side closer to you, tightly roll with your fingers. Then use the bamboo mat and cover roll, gently squeezing firmly to compact roll.
5. Place a sheet of plastic wrap on the counter. Spread tempura crumbs onto the sheet; add roll and coat thoroughly with crumbs. Cover roll with the plastic wrap, and slice with a sharp damp knife into 8 pieces, each approximately 1-inch thick.
6. Remove the plastic wrap and plate. Top with drizzle of eel sauce.

Vegetable Roll

The Vegetable Roll is a free for all with your favorite vegetables.

½ sheet *nori*, approximately 4×7-inches

¾ cup prepared sushi rice

Sesame seeds, as needed

2 green lettuce leaves

2 pieces broccoli, steamed, approximately 3-inches long

1 pickled gobo root (a.k.a. mountain burdock or *yamagobo*), whole

1 slice avocado

2 slender strips cucumber, approximately 4-inches long with skin

1 or 2 slices vine-ripe tomato

Daikon radish sprouts *(kaiware)*, approximately 12 strands

Serving size: 5 or 6 slices

Note: Feel free to use any of your favorite vegetables.

1. Place nori in front of you, in a vertical position, shiny side down.
2. Spoon rice onto nori. Using your fingers, spread rice, covering edges and smoothing clumps. Leave 1-inch space with no rice at top. Sprinkle rice with sesame seeds.
3. Place lettuce leaves in lower portion of sheet. Along side, add broccoli, gobo root, avocado, cucumber, tomato, and radish sprouts with petals hanging over edges outside roll.
4. Start at side closer to you, and tightly roll with your fingers. Use the bamboo mat and cover roll, gently squeezing firmly to compact roll.
5. Using a sharp damp knife, slice roll into 5 or 6 pieces and plate.

From the Kitchen

Like the Tropical Roll, experiment with other vegetables and see what you like best. Other vegetable choices that work well in this roll include: asparagus, bell pepper, cabbage, carrots, cauliflower and fresh spinach.

Chapter 10

Appetizers and Salads

In This Chapter

- Ten creative appetizers and salads
- Kitchen pointers
- Selecting the perfect garnish

When entertaining guests, it's always nice to start off with a few exceptional snacks before the main course. Below are some delicious appetizer and salad ideas that will leave your guests craving more and eager to try anything that comes next. These fun and creative dishes will definitely be the talk of your party. Start off by serving delicious volcano rolls while your guests are mingling about. Once everyone is seated around the table, serve a unique salad, like the salmon skin salad or the spicy jellyfish salad with endive, smelt eggs and avocado. A word of warning, however: it will be difficult to keep everyone from filling up on these savory starters.

Always remember, the fresher the ingredients, the better tasting your dishes will be. Whenever possible, select fresh, never frozen, and ripe instead of unripe.

Cucumber Salad Roll

Start off a dinner party by serving your guests this seafood enriched roll.

Serving Size: 5 to 6 slices

2 shrimp

½ English cucumber, peeled

4 pieces salmon or tuna, thinly sliced, approximately 1×4-inches

3 TB. crab mixture (recipe in Chapter 7)

1 TB. smelt eggs or flying fish roe

1 medium-size slice avocado

Daikon radish sprouts *(kaiware)*, approximately 12 strands

Ponzu sauce, as needed (recipe in Chapter 7)

Sesame seeds, as needed

1. Prepare shrimp by sliding a metal or bamboo skewer through length of tail sections with shell on to prohibit tails from curling when cooked. Place the skewer in a pot of boiling water until tails are pink and tender. Immediately dip shrimp into an ice water bath to stop the cooking process. Remove shrimp from the skewer, discard shells, and butterfly. Set aside.
2. With a sharp knife, carefully slice cucumber like peeling an apple, creating one long continuous slice. Take your time as this requires patience and perfection.
3. Lay long, thin cucumber out in front of you in a vertical position.
4. Working from bottom of cucumber sheet, add salmon slices, shrimp, crab mixture, roe, avocado, and radish sprouts.
5. Roll sheet tightly with your fingers, beginning with end closer to you.
6. Using a sharp damp knife, slice roll into 5 or 6 slices, and arrange on a plate. Top with drizzle of ponzu sauce and sprinkle of sesame seeds.

Creamy Sesame Dressing

So much flavor for so few ingredients.

Serving Size: 2

2 TB. ground sesame seeds

1 tsp. rice vinegar

1 tsp. vegetable oil

1 tsp. sugar

1 tsp. soy sauce

1 to 2 tsp. mayonnaise

1. Mix sesame seeds, vinegar, oil, sugar, soy sauce, and mayonnaise in a bowl, and chill until ready to serve.

Ebi Fried Shrimp

This is perfect finger food to pass around at any gathering.

Servings: 1 to 2 persons

4 large shrimp or prawns, cleaned, shelled, and deveined

3 cups vegetable oil

1 cup flour for dusting

2 eggs, beaten

1 cup breadcrumbs

2 cups cabbage, chopped

Creamy sesame dressing, as needed (recipe in this chapter)

1. With a sharp knife, butterfly shrimp, being careful not to sever halves. Heat oil over high heat in a deep fryer, pot, or pan.
2. Dip each shrimp in flour and shake off excess. Next, dip in egg, then breadcrumbs, coating well.
3. Carefully place each battered shrimp into hot oil and deep fry until crisp and golden brown. Remove and let rest on a paper towel.
4. On a serving plate, mound cabbage in the center and arrange fried shrimp on top.
5. Drizzle with creamy sesame dressing.

Variation: Scallops make an excellent alternative. Buy large sea scallops, and slice in half lengthwise to speed up the deep-frying process.

From the Kitchen

In Japanese, fried shrimp is called ebi-fry. Besides breadcrumbs, you can also coat your shrimp in Panko (Japanese bread crumbs).

Hawaiian Poke

This traditional salad will leave your guests asking for the recipe.

Servings: 1 to 2 persons

1 cup diced ahi-grade tuna

¼ cup maui onion, thinly sliced

Salt and pepper to taste

2 TB. cucumber, thinly sliced with skin

2 TB. daikon radish sprouts *(kaiware)*, cut in half

3 or 4 TB. mixed seaweed, (marinated *wakame*)

½ TB. smelt eggs or flying fish roe

½ TB. soy sauce

½ TB. sesame oil

Sesame seeds, as needed

1. In a bowl, toss tuna, onion, salt and pepper, cucumber, radish sprouts, seaweed, roe, soy sauce, and sesame oil until well incorporated. Transfer to a serving plate, and sprinkle top with sesame seeds.

Japanese Sea Bass with Garlic Soy Sauce

The powerful flavor of this sauce will highlight the more subtle aspects of the sea bass.

Servings: 1 to 2 persons

1 or 2 large shiitake mushrooms, sliced

1 piece fresh sea bass, approximately 1×4-inches, ½-inch thick

1 garlic clove, thinly sliced

1 asparagus spear, sliced in long pieces on the diagonal

1 small handful of enoki mushrooms

1 block of tofu, approximately 2×4-inches, 1-inch thick

Sesame seeds, as needed

For Sauce:

2 TB. sesame oil

1 clove garlic, sliced

2 TB. soy sauce

2 TB. cooking sake

2 TB. water

Pinch scallions

1 or 2 dashes chili powder

1. To make sauce: In a saucepan over medium heat, add oil and cook garlic until soften and golden. Add soy sauce, sake, and water. Stir well. Add scallions and chili powder. Stir again, and let cook for several minutes. Remove from heat and reserve.
2. On a baking sheet lined with foil, arrange shiitake mushrooms and set sea bass alongside. Top bass with garlic. Alongside bass, add asparagus.
3. Drizzle mushrooms, bass, and asparagus liberally with Garlic Soy Sauce.
4. Place the sheet in a toaster oven or under the broiler for 4 to 5 minutes or until bass is half-cooked.

5. Add enoki mushrooms alongside asparagus. Cook until fish is opaque and tender, and remove from heat.
6. Meanwhile, heat tofu by either microwaving or submerging in a pot of boiling water.
7. When thoroughly heated, place tofu block in the center of a large serving plate. Place bass with garlic atop tofu. Spoon shiitake mushrooms over bass. Lean asparagus and enoki mushrooms against tofu and sea bass. Drizzle with remaining cooking juices, and finish with sprinkle of sesame seeds.

Fish Facts

Be careful when selecting sea bass. Chilean Sea Bass is a trade name for the Patagonian Toothfish which is greatly overfished. In fact, more than half of all Patagonian Toothfish sold are caught illegally.

Mango Salmon

The Mango Salmon is the perfect appetizer to start a romantic evening.

Servings: 1 to 2 persons

2 TB. maui onion or sweet or red onion

3 thin slices of salmon, approximately 2×3-inches

Daikon radish sprouts *(kaiware)*, approximately 12 strands, cut in half

Mango sauce (recipe follows)

Smelt eggs or flying fish roe, as needed

Sesame seeds, as needed

1. Thinly slice onion, and divide into 3 equal parts. Top each salmon slice with onion.
2. Roll each salmon slice with your fingers, and cut in half with a sharp, damp knife.
3. Arrange 6 sliced salmon rolls on a plate and top with radish sprouts.
4. Top each roll with dollop of mango sauce, sprinkle of smelt eggs or flying fish roe, and sesame seeds.

Mango Sauce

To make them a little sweeter, add mango sauce to any salmon sushi roll.

1 ripe mango, peeled and diced

$\frac{1}{4}$ oz. rice vinegar

1 oz. cooking sake or light rum

1 TB. sugar

1 TB. mayonnaise

Pinch salt

1 tsp. soy sauce

1. In a blender, pulverize mango until smooth. Add vinegar, sake or rum, sugar, mayonnaise, salt, and soy sauce, and blend until incorporated.

Red Sea Urchin *Uni* Shooter

Those more familiar with sushi often add sake to this recipe.

Servings: 1 shooter

2 to 3 pieces fresh sea urchin *(Uni)*

½ oz. Ponzu sauce

1 quail egg (yolk only)

Pinch of finely sliced scallion (damp dry with paper towel)

½ TB. chili daikon (equal parts of bottled chili sauce mixed with finely diced daikon radish sprouts).

1. Fill a shot glass ½ full with ponzu sauce. For homemade ponzu: mix equal parts of lemon juice, rice vinegar, water, sake, and pinch of dry seaweed (optional).
2. Add 2 to 3 pieces of fresh urchin roe. Add egg yolk, and top off with pinch of scallions and chili daikon.

Fish Facts

Not only is uni a Japanese delicacy, but the unique ingredient is a highly prized item—very much like caviar—in such places as Chile, Greece, Lebanon, Korea and Spain.

Salmon Skin Salad

Top this salad with a light vinegar dressing.

Servings: 1 to 2 persons

1 sheet salmon skin, approximately 3×5-inches

3 TB. cucumber, thinly sliced with skin

1 large pinch daikon radish sprouts (*kai-ware*)

2 TB. mixed seaweed, (marinated *wakame*)

½ TB. smelt eggs or flying fish roe

Sesame seeds, as needed

Seven-spice chili powder (*shichimi toga-rashi)*, to taste

1 TB. Ponzu sauce (recipe in Chapter 7)

1 pickled gobo root, thinly sliced

½ TB. *katsuobushi* (dried shaved fish flakes)

1. Prepare salmon skin by removing section of skin approximately 3×5-inches from fresh salmon filet. Sprinkle skin with salt, and roast in a toaster oven or under the broiler until skin is crispy. Remove from heat, and finely chop with a knife.
2. In a bowl, add salmon skin, cucumber, radish sprouts, seaweed, roe, sesame seeds, chili powder, ponzu sauce, and gobo root. Toss well to coat.
3. Place salad in the center of a serving dish, and top with shaved fish flakes.

Soft Shell Crab

The Eastern version of a Western favorite.

Servings: 1 person

1 soft shell crab

Corn starch, for dusting

Hot oil, for deep-frying

Dipping Sauce:

2 or 3 TB. Ponzu sauce (recipe in Chapter 7)

Pinch of chili daikon

Pinch of finely chopped scallions

1. Dust crab in corn starch and shake off excess.
2. Deep-fry crab in hot oil until golden brown.
3. Remove crab from oil and plate immediately.
4. Serve with the dipping sauce, by combining Ponzu sauce, chili daikon, and finely chopped scallions.

Spicy Jellyfish Salad with Endive, Smelt Eggs, and Avocado

This unique and satisfying salad is perfect for the health savvy.

Serving Size: 1 salad

2 oz. chopped jellyfish (lengthwise)

Daikon radish sprouts *(kaiware)*, approximately 12 strands

Small bunch (10 to 12 leaves) fresh spinach

¼ chopped sweet onion (white or red)

1 large pinch green onions or scallions, thinly sliced like matchsticks

2 TB. cucumber, thinly sliced like matchsticks

1 fried wanton skin

Salt and pepper to taste

Olive oil, as needed

Sesame seeds, as needed

½ tsp. smelt eggs or flying fish roe

For garnish:

4 endive leaves

1 avocado, sliced

2 TB. smelt eggs or flying fish roe.

1. Mix together jellyfish, *kaiware*, spinach, onion, scallions, and cucumber. Add salt, pepper, and olive oil.
2. Deep fry wanton skin, and place in center of a dish.
3. Place large scoop of salad inside wanton skin. On top, add smelt eggs, and sprinkle sesame seeds over salad.

4. To garnish, add endive around salad. Inside each leaf, place avocado slice and smelt eggs.

Food Corner

Because prepared jellyfish is approximately 95-percent water and 4 to 5-percent protein, this unique seafood item is a relatively low calorie food.

Tiger Eye

The display of this dish is as appealing as the taste.

Serving size: 7 to 8 pieces

½ sheet *nori*, approximately 4×7-inches

1 to 2 TB. prepared sushi rice

5 to 6 thin slices salmon, approximately 1-inch wide and 4-inches long

1 fresh calamari steak, approximately 3×4-inches.

1 medium-size slice avocado

1 cup fried rice noodles

Eel sauce, as needed (recipe in Chapter 7)

Sesame seeds, as needed

1. Place nori in front of you, in a vertical position, shiny side down.
2. Layer nori with salmon slices. Stagger pieces while working from bottom to top. Leave about 2-inches empty at top of sheet.
3. Fill space at top with rice, covering edges. Center avocado slice over salmon. Start at the bottom and tightly roll with your fingers. Set aside.
4. With a sharp, damp knife, insert the blade into side of calamari steak and open center creating a large pouch. Do not cut the ends. Place roll inside calamari pouch.
5. Place calamari roll onto a baking sheet lined with foil. Cook in a toaster oven or under the broiler for 3 to 4 minutes. Turn roll over, and cook for another 2 to 3 minutes. Do not overcook, as calamari will be chewy and tough.
6. Remove roll, and using the sharp, damp knife, slice into 7 to 8 pieces.
7. On a plate, place mound of rice noodles in the center. Arrange roll slices on noodles, and finish with drizzle of Eel sauce and sprinkle of sesame seeds.

Volcano Roll

To feel the true fire of a Volcano Roll, substitute some of the ingredients with their spicy counterparts.

Servings: 5 to 6 pieces

½ sheet *nori*, approximately 4×7-inches

6 to 7 thin slices salmon, approximately 1×4-inches

¾ cup prepared sushi rice

Sesame seeds, as needed

2 thin slices halibut, approximately 1×4-inches

1 or 2 TB. crab mixture (recipe in Chapter 7)

1 thin slice avocado

½ TB. smelt eggs or flying fish roe

1 cup mayonnaise

1 TB. raw egg

2 TB. finely chopped scallion

Eel sauce, as needed (recipe in Chapter 7)

1. Place nori in front of you, in a vertical position, shiny side down.
2. Layer nori with salmon, covering entire sheet.
3. Place a sheet of plastic wrap onto the counter, and flip seaweed sheet over onto the plastic, salmon side down. Spoon rice onto seaweed, and using your fingers, spread rice evenly, covering edges and smoothing clumps. Sprinkle rice with sesame seeds.
4. Add halibut to lower half of seaweed. Add crab mixture onto halibut, followed by avocado and smelt eggs or roe.
5. Starting from lower end, tightly roll with your fingers, keeping the plastic wrap on the outside. Using the bamboo mat, cover roll and gently squeeze firmly to compact.

5. Keeping the plastic wrap intact, slice roll (through the plastic) with a sharp, damp knife into 5 to 6 pieces, each approximately 1-inch thick. Arrange slices on a baking sheet lined with foil.
6. Combine mayonnaise with egg. Top each slice with 1 TB. mayonnaise mixture.
7. Place the baking sheet in a toaster oven or under the broiler until mayonnaise topping is golden brown.
8. Remove and arrange on a plate. Top with finely chopped scallion, Eel sauce, spicy sauce, and sesame seeds.

Food Corner

In Texas, a variation of the Volcano Roll is made with a hot scallop mixture, along with smelt roe, wasabi, pickled ginger and lemon.

Index

D

E

F

L

M

N-O

P

T

U-V

W-X-Y-Z

The *fun* cookbook library

978-1-59257-576-3

978-1-59257-484-1

978-1-59257-658-6

978-1-59257-318-9

978-1-59257-737-8

978-1-59257-674-6

978-1-59257-699-9

Check out these and more than 20 other cooking titles from *The Complete Idiot's Guides*®!